Innovation and Knowledge Communities

Innovation and Knowledge Communities
The Hidden Structure of Technology

Phin Upham

Managing Partner, Haymaker Ventures, USA

EE Edward Elgar
PUBLISHING

Cheltenham, UK • Northampton, MA, USA

Published by
Edward Elgar Publishing Limited
The Lypiatts
15 Lansdown Road
Cheltenham
Glos GL50 2JA
UK

Edward Elgar Publishing, Inc.
William Pratt House
9 Dewey Court
Northampton
Massachusetts 01060
USA

A catalogue record for this book
is available from the British Library

This book is available electronically in the **Elgar**online
Business subject collection
http://dx.doi.org/10.4337/9781800371835

Printed on elemental chlorine free (ECF)
recycled paper containing 30% Post-Consumer Waste

ISBN 978 1 80037 182 8 (cased)
ISBN 978 1 80037 183 5 (eBook)

Printed and bound in the USA

Contents

v

1. Introduction

During the COVID-19 pandemic, many people were kept far away from colleagues, co-authors, and co-founders, but their work continued via video conferencing, smart phones, and email—something that would not have been possible only decades ago. From the printing press to the Internet, technology has long helped conquer the tyranny of distance and time. Increasingly, this is true not only for sharing ideas but also for creating them. Innovation in science and technology is becoming an asynchronous conversation across time, geographies, organizations, and disciplines. Existing frameworks for how these innovations occur, however, are mired in language about cities, countries, companies, founders, and universities.

Scientific and technological progress is increasingly the result of a profoundly collaborative endeavor—split between innovators in the private and the public sectors, large companies and startups, universities and technology hubs, colleagues and strangers, and those near and far. The stories we tell about such innovation in both the academic literature and popular discourse do not capture these rich interactions well. Research in academia and management consulting too often ends up commodifying innovation—focusing on generic "firms" and modeling them as machine-like entities to be studied in terms of internal dynamics and key differences. Popular narratives in the press, even in Silicon Valley, are too eager to find a hero—focusing only on the de novo, singular brilliance of a technical founder, engineer, or small team of scientists.

An underappreciated and understudied part of innovation in science and technology is the contribution of spontaneous clusters of researchers, scientists, and thinkers, around the world, working on a common project, united by common purpose, not connected by organizational or other affiliation. Such rich and generative environments today have critical social dimensions that are hidden in plain sight. Indeed, the most important teams in the world of science and technology may already be teams of strangers. Much of the key work in innovation for technical fields is not coordinated by universities, governments, big tech, or any other formal institutions. This is the phenomenon we seek to better understand.

The special power of informal collaboration between researchers is an old idea, often traced to Bernard of Chartres in the twelfth century and known best in the words of Sir Isaac Newton: "If I have seen further, it is by standing on the shoulders of giants." Such collaboration has expanded exponentially with the advent of the Internet, the digitalization of knowledge, and the globalization of research and technology. Modern evangelists of blockchain envision a decentralized Web3 version of the Internet rebuilt on such non-hierarchical networks and governed via shared rules. But until the last few decades, the technology did not exist to study such broad collaboration or understand it systematically. Recently, however, technologies developed to, for example, cluster similar web pages and analyze massive quantities of data, like bioinformatics of gene expression, allow us to anecdotally recognize the importance of informal collaboration and to systematically study the mechanisms that lead to success. Perhaps someday we can even learn how to encourage such interactions to accelerate innovation.

In some rare, special cases, the work of a group of loosely associated innovators, working collectively but not together, assumes a sort of joint coherency. The group begins to function as if it were a new emergent organizational form—capable of very productive collaboration. We refer to this phenomenon as a "knowledge community." While it is not exclusive to innovation in science and technology, we think it is particularly prevalent there. Scientific or technological knowledge communities comprise an interorganizational large-scale network in which researchers work together by building on each other's advances—whether in an approach to cancer research, a new microchip, or a COVID-19 vaccine. In the for-profit realm, these communities often form in times of urgency, technological breakthrough, or existential need—when sharing ideas quickly trumps keeping them proprietary, and good ideas are more important than firm borders.

These knowledge communities are an exemplar of the social process we are studying. Many studies suggest that researchers in such unstructured research clusters or communities tend to produce at much higher rates of innovation than either less cohesive researchers or more structured teams. But rarely has research taken such knowledge communities as central, not only to the success of specific innovations, but to the continued success of the processes that generate those innovations.

The implications of thinking about networks of innovators who share ideas instead of formal organizations (like companies, governments, universities, or nonprofits) are profound— indeed, we find that unusual organizing logics guide such informal research clusters. Existing anecdotal research suggests, to generalize very broadly, that organizations such as technology firms seek to combine diverse specialties and to coordinate deeply heterogeneous tasks—such as marketing, finance, management, and production—toward a set of goals. To generalize again, networks, such as knowledge communities, however, tend toward homogeneity by gathering together people with similar ideas where they can learn from and build upon each other's work. How these two different patterns of influence and innovation overlay each other in dynamic tension in the real world, where both exist simultaneously, is particularly salient in arenas such as R&D and technology.

Examining the interplay between organizational boundaries and knowledge flow reveals interesting and counterintuitive lessons about identifying promising innovations as they emerge. How do successful knowledge creators, CEOs, and corporate R&D researchers engage in communal knowledge development and simultaneously maintain proprietary knowledge? Understanding this would inform the corporate and scientific use of patents, internal knowledge development, and more generally the way companies might identify and take advantage of innovation and change. Since we find that areas of innovation often originate in such decentralized intellectual communities, it may be advantageous for firms to identify them as they emerge in order to benefit from their good ideas, to monitor the risks and rewards of investing in a community or an idea, and to be better aware of how their scientists are interacting with knowledge communities. Indeed, this is precisely how the innovations that underpin Google originated.

THEORY AND DATA

Network theory over the past several decades has revealed the difference interpersonal network ties make, and how crucial they are to social structures. Seminal network theorists James Coleman and Ron Burt challenged traditional views about what determines outcomes—demographic attributes, such as class, age, and strength—with network-based ideas, such as network centrality, social capital, and structural holes (Burt, 2000). Network theorists argued that, in many cases, outcomes are determined not chiefly by what you know, but instead by whom you know and how you are connected to others. Later network researchers, such as Harrison White, Mark Granovetter, and more recently Duncan Watts, have built on these ideas by showing that the structure of relationships does matter, not only in a given situation but also on the larger scale of social structure—which they see as comprising interpersonal/internode relationships writ large (Burt, 1977; Granovetter, 1994; Jacobs & Watts, 2021; Watts, 1999; White, 2003).

We use data to identify and understand, at least on some level, these intense clusters of innovators that we call knowledge communities. The challenge, formally speaking, in researching this new informal model of collaboration, is to infer the social structure of knowledge from the content of interactions. This book looks at the use of shared knowledge, or shared rhetoric, as the unit of agglomeration for the social structure of knowledge. In our data context—citations and language in scientific and social science publications—content is more apparent and accessible. Therefore, rather than inferring content from connections, we infer connections from content. These connections, or ties, however, are not friendship ties, or even necessarily acquaintanceship ties, but exchanges of ideas (or proxies for them, at least). We show how ideas are tied together into knowledge communities and how their position in these communities has consequences for their impact.

The difficulty of finding and interpreting the content of interactions is increasingly reduced by technologies, such as email and inexpensive electronic storage, which have opened up new avenues for content analysis. One very promising area for exploration is the systematic compilation of text and citations in shared academic discourse, such as the sciences and social sciences, which is where we focus our efforts (Small, 1992, 1998, 2018b; Upham, Rosenkopf, & Ungar, 2010a, 2010b; Upham & Small, 2010). In other words, we use techniques in network analysis to study the content of interactions and the social structure implied by that content.

Scientific and academic discourse are of special interest because of particular attributes in this arena and the more public way in which ideas are exchanged. Three aspects of scientific articles are particularly useful: First, published articles in the sciences and social sciences describe the researcher's own positions. Second, published articles include citations through which the author acknowledges the influence of the knowledge and ideas of others. Third, these published articles can themselves be cited, becoming a part of this social discourse of ideas. The same is true for patent research, though secrecy and legal considerations make this context somewhat more complex.

The formal work of scientists and technologists—their papers, patents, and inventions—becomes their primary source of professional self-identification and in turn helps shape their intellectual community (Hargens, 2000b; McCain, 1986a; Parker & Corte, 2017; Schardosin et al., 2020). The printed page or, increasingly, the computer screen is where scientists interact. Before the Internet and long-distance telephony, scholars around the world rarely, if ever, met, interacting via the printed page. Scientists are not, in other words, intellectually defined so much by with whom they have lunch as by with whom they agree intellectually and on whose innovations and work they build (Merton, 1965). Of course, the social structure in intellectual communities can be complemented by personal interactions at conferences and universities. Nevertheless, scientists are often more similar, in terms of discipline, knowledge and ideas, to someone with whom they agree intellectually and have never met than they are to the researcher across the hall (Collins, 1997). In other words, in technical domains, it is often their knowledge community, not just their organization, that shapes a person's innovations (Zhang et al., 2020).

SUMMARY

This book attempts to study the interaction between knowledge communities and organizational boundaries in different contexts, in order to better understand how they intersect in practice. We focus on three communities of innovators and examine, in each, different aspects of how knowledge is exchanged and how broad collaboration has changed old knowledge-sharing paradigms. In three chapters, we emphasize the content of interactions and their effect on performance by examining citations in academic and scientific papers. We also focus on the methodology of clustering in order to find intellectual communities formed on the basis of ideas and beliefs. Finally, we focus on the importance of considering method in evaluating the coherency and validity of knowledge communities (Upham, 2006; Upham, Rosenkopf, & Ungar, 2010a).

We study, in Chapter 2, the field of computer science over more than a decade. We ask how computer scientists organize themselves into cohesive knowledge communities and how these communities help their members to succeed or fail (Upham, Rosenkopf, & Ungar, 2010b). In this field, there is a good deal of direct involvement from the private sector, and many discoveries have led directly to entrepreneurial and business applications (Ma & Uzzi, 2018; Popescul et al., 2000). Computer science as an area of research is a "dual economy," where incentives to publish and generate publicly useful information can coexist with the incentive to use information in a proprietary way to gain direct market returns (Gittelman & Kogut, 2003). That science and industry are more directly intertwined in this context yields an interesting angle for analysis.

As we step back to examine the way in which knowledge communities interact with each other, we begin to examine patterns and develop explanations for their differential performance—explanations that differ significantly from intuitions developed from looking at interactions between formal organizations. These knowledge communities are not led by a CEO or president; they do not have an official name or organizational structure. They exist, rather, as a reflection of the substantiveness of their members' knowledge-sharing behavior—the cohesiveness of their shared content. There is a tension between the way these communities use knowledge and the way they generate rhetoric—a tension that is irresolvable because these two aspects of knowledge communities are intertwined and yet pull in orthogonal directions.

Little work has looked at what drives the relative performance of knowledge communities and indirectly, therefore, the relative progress of science. Understanding knowledge communities is essential to understanding progress, and might be centrally important to scientific researchers and firms investing in R&D (Jones, 2021). We compare the knowledge content and the rhetorical content of each of these knowledge communities to see if we can find a basis for differential success. We find that the way knowledge communities learn from particular knowledge as a foundation and the way they generate knowledge as rhetoric to introduce new ideas have opposite tendencies, and are under strong and constant tension. In successful knowledge communities, knowledge content is drawn from a broad range of sources and is extremely flexible. In contrast, successful communities tend to use very similar rhetoric, their rhetorical content tends to remain central over time, and it tends not to be unique or esoteric when compared to the vocabulary of other communities.

In Chapter 3, we conduct a type of meta-analysis on corporate strategy itself, the very field we are hoping to challenge (Upham et al., 2010a). If we can show that even researchers obsessed with organizations are themselves often driven (at least in part) by their intense membership to knowledge communities, we hope to have accomplished a sort of research Judo. We focus on how researchers position their ideas in and between knowledge communities to maximize their impact and success. Management strategists tend to share their knowledge with each other and with practitioners quite freely. In this field, ideas are hard to patent, and the social uptake of ideas and their success are directly intertwined (Abrahamson, 1996; Eccles, Nohria, & Berkley, 1992; Meyer, 1999; Ponzi, 2002).

Using a clustering methodology developed for this work, we look at the structure of the field's intellectual content and how publishing authors interact in patterns with one another (Hotelling, 1929). We study how the impact of published papers differs depending on how the authors position their papers within and between knowledge communities, which are defined intellectual communities.

We find that it is significantly beneficial for new knowledge to be a part of a knowledge community and also that, within a knowledge community, new knowledge has much more impact if it is in the intellectual semi-periphery, rather than at its periphery or center. This implies a curvilinear relationship within a knowledge community between a work's range of citations and impact. Further, we find some conflicting evidence about whether working in multiple schools of thought results in higher impact. We also show that the conclusions we draw in this chapter and the previous one, each in a different context, apply to both of the datasets. We hope this helps generalize our conclusions and, statistically at least, increase the robustness of our findings.

In Chapter 4, where we use emerging clusters in the hard sciences and basic research, we begin to explore the mechanisms by which knowledge changes over time, with the foundations of innovation and technology: basic research (Small & Upham, 2009; Upham & Small, 2010). We study the most technical fields where so many new scientific ideas percolate first. While this research has the potential to be commercialized (leading to the value of proprietary knowledge), at least in the U.S.A. and Europe as dominant geographies for patents and scientific research, research is still largely federally funded and, overall, the framework of shared basic science still dominates (Gulovsen, 2019; Ma & Uzzi, 2018; Murray & Stern, 2005).

We determine the areas of science that have the most cohesive high-intensity innovation, which we call "emerging fronts." For these fronts, we interview experts in the scientific community to verify our quantitative findings. We begin to consider how a citation structure within scientific research can reveal the processes of change within intellectual communities and how new research emerges into prominence from existing knowledge, potentially to break away and become a distinct field of knowledge itself.

Emerging fronts of research represent the very beginnings of new and cohesive micro-revolutions in science, something only a few have attempted to study systematically at this stage. We select highly cited and cohesive sets of research, which represent the emergence of fresh and potentially important innovations. The insights gained by our qualitative interviews are used to test the success of our method and to contribute to future attempts to identify emerging fronts of research.

The research sources used by these fronts can help us identify patterns. We look at cross-disciplinary research to see if there is a pattern of increased interdisciplinary research among these high-impact clusters over the past five years. Academic research in the sciences has been shown to not only generate important "basic" research that is used by scientists and researchers, but also to have significant spillover into the private sector.

A NEW DAWN

Technology has long been a driver of change and disruption, and the rise of decentralized, dynamic knowledge communities is no exception. The Internet allows sharing and collaboration on a scale never before seen; it should be of no surprise therefore that it has impacted the process of innovation itself. While geographic technology clusters, like Silicon Valley and research universities, like MIT or Harvard, play an enormous part in furthering knowledge, it is also important to understand how they are drawing on and interacting with broad research efforts in other fields, regions, and institutions. Blockchain technology means that decentralized communities and DAOs may not require intermediation by formal organizations. Innovation has gone global; a new invisible set of informal networks have formed that will drive its pace and direction. Clustering technologies provide a window into this phenomenon that could prove to be valuable in understanding how innovation happens in a modern, connected world—and how to potentially help it flourish.

Most of the scarce existing literature on knowledge communities (often described in different terms, such as paradigms, clusters, or invisible colleges) has focused on describing the phenomenon rather than how it works and how it emerges and evolves, or why it is accelerating. Little research has looked at what features in a knowledge community increase innovation rates over time. In this book, we begin this task by first constructing a robust clustering methodology and then trying to tease out and test the characteristics that allow knowledge communities to succeed. We then study what incentive structures exist for individuals to join and grow their respective knowledge communities. Lastly, we explore how powerful new ideas are "born" in emerging fronts and what characteristics allow them to gain intellectual coherence in their early days, eventually potentially becoming larger knowledge communities.

Innovation and technology are working on fundamentally different principles than before innovators, scientists, and others could share information so broadly and instantaneously with others they did not know and might never meet. This has resulted in the need to rethink the importance of formal firm boundaries, in favor of a network perspective of knowledge.

As is so often the case, the whole "tree" may have been contained within the tiny "acorn" and inevitable from the start—the very first internet in the world, the ARPANET, was formed to link Pentagon-funded research institutions and to accelerate research collaboration. We are excited about how a better understanding of decentralized knowledge communities can accelerate innovation and technology.

2. Innovating knowledge communities: an analysis of group collaboration and competition in science and technology

INTRODUCTION AND THEORY

The study of innovation has largely focused on formal organizations, usually firms. But the advent of the Internet and the acceleration of knowledge sharing is increasingly making collaboration between researchers at different firms important for progress. We believe that researchers that communicate between their organizations provide a major source of new ideas and extraordinary value for them—and we want to understand how this interorganizational interaction might function (Crane 1972, 1989; Fleming & Sorenson, 2001; Kuhn, 1962; Small, 2003). As previously argued, in some special cases, a group of researchers, united by an area of mutual interest, form an informal cluster or "knowledge community" that has an intellectual and social coherency. Such knowledge communities can exist in any specialized areas of research where there is free exchange of information—looking for a cure for Alzheimer's disease, trying to improve Internet search or looking to improve the gas efficiency of diesel engines (Culnan, 1986; Guimera et al., 2005; Hargens, 2000a; Jung, Kim, & Kim, 2019; Schardosin et al., 2020; Small, 1994).

Formal organizations (like firms, startups, or government agencies) and knowledge communities (spontaneous clusters of researchers collaborating) are fundamentally different in several ways that are not intuitive. Research suggests that formal organizations are extremely effective coordinating bodies, internalizing arm's-length transactions by bringing together numerous heterogeneous specialties (marketing, research, management, sales, etc.) and, when successful, imposing a vertically organized, unified incentive structure to maximize a goal or set of goals (Williamson, 1975, 1988, 2017). We all know that firms are more complex and messier than this, but this is probably a good enough generalization. In contrast, knowledge communities are by their very nature homogenous, unifying people of similar research interests and specialties to learn from each other and build on each other's ideas (Merton, 1972). Indeed, members of knowledge communities can work together as closely as the members of most firms, yet may never meet (Crane, 1989). While firms are excellent at facilitating cooperation by unifying incentives, knowledge communities are superb at encouraging collaboration; this embodies the distinction between working together and working jointly.

Being part of a knowledge community has many advantages for researchers (and studies of cross-disciplinary work show the potential difficulties of working outside or between knowledge communities [Amir, 1985; Birnbaum, 1981a, 1981c]). An interactive knowledge community offers a built-in and knowledgeable audience for research, a stimulating intellectual dialogue, and an accelerated technical environment (Crane, 1972, 1989; Kuhn, 1962). Being a member of a knowledge community is less of a conscious choice than a reflection of being a part of a stream of knowledge that involves the collaboration and cooperation of other researchers in a tight, cohesive pattern of research.

In this chapter, we examine two aspects of knowledge communities: how they use and build on previous knowledge, and how they use language (Abrahamson, 1996; Antons et al., 2020; Braam, Moed, & Vanraan, 1991a, 1991b). The knowledge communities we study work primarily by publishing papers on a technical subject—computer science—in journals or by presenting papers in conferences. Their goal is to disseminate knowledge about discoveries that a member of the community has made (Garfield, 1983, 1988). Citations in papers, like citations in patents, are made when other work has been influential in a discovery (Merton, 1965).

What are the key structural factors that drive a knowledge community's success? We attempt to quantify some of the substantive differences between knowledge communities in how they use both previous knowledge and rhetoric. First, we examine *community cohesiveness*, or the extent to which communities build on each other's knowledge and language. Next, we examine *community uniqueness*, or the extent to which a knowledge community is different from others in its use of past knowledge and language. Finally, we examine *community flexibility*, or the rate of change a knowledge community has shown over time in its use of knowledge and language. Despite the importance of successful knowledge communities for technical progress, mainstream management research has not studied what creates them, particularly those that are not geographically based. We draw on two emerging areas of network research that have examined innovation in large-scale networks, though with different emphases: research on small worlds, and research on geographic technology clusters.

Duncan Watts's work on "small worlds" (Watts, 1999) builds on Stanley Milgram's discussion of "6 degrees of separation" (Milgram, 1967; Travers & Milgram, 1969). Watts observed that the aggregate structure of connections between people and other networks was not random. Rather, tight clusters of relationships were connected by less frequent bridging relationships between clusters (Watts, 1999). This allowed for the "short tie" advantages of a cohesive community as well as the "long tie" benefits of recombination between ideas from different communities (Fleming, Mingo, & Chen, 2005). These ideas have begun to allow network theorists to effectively grapple with large-scale networks of all sorts. For example, Brian Uzzi studies the small world of the casts of Broadway musicals, arguing that this structure allows for a "cradle of creativity" between tight clusters with repeated interactions and some fresh new ideas drawn from less familiar connections (Guimera et al., 2005; Uzzi & Spiro, 2005):

> Creativity is not only, as myth tells, the brash work of loners, but also the consequence of a social system of actors that amplify or stifle one another's creativity … the creativity of many key figures, including Beethoven, Thomas Hutchinson, David Hume, Adam Smith, Cosimo de'Medici, Erasmus Darwin (inventor and naturalist father of Charles Darwin), and famed bassist Jamie Jamison—who, as a permanent member of the Funk Brothers, cowrote more number one hit songs than the Beatles, the Rolling Stones, the Beach Boys, and Elvis combined … all abided by the same pattern of being embedded in a network of artists or scientists who shared ideas and acted as both critics and fans for each other. (Uzzi & Spiro, 2005, p. 448)

Michael Porter and others have argued for a different logic behind such communities of expertise. They study geographic clusters of competence, showing how a bubble of geographically close, dense connections, high expert knowledge, and unified interests has led to sustained advantages in innovation and core competencies (Delgado & Porter, 2021; Porter, 1998; Porter et al., 2004). Porter explains:

> Clusters represent a kind of new special organizational form in between arm's length markets on the one hand and hierarchies, or vertical integration, on the other. A cluster, then, is an alternative way of organizing the value chain. Compared with market transactions among dispersed and random buyers and sellers, the proximity of companies and institutions in one location—and the repeated exchanges among them—fosters better coordination and trust … A cluster of independent and informally linked companies and institutions represents a robust organizational form that offers advantages in efficiency, effectiveness, and flexibility. (Porter, 1998, pp. 79–80)

This strain of thought assumes that communities are geographical, like Silicon Valley in the 1990s, and that it is the social reinforcement, and in some sense external dislocation, of people into the "bubble" that allows for such effective innovation in business (Aharonson, Baum, & Feldman, 2004; Kerr & Robert-Nicoud, 2020). At first a gathering of convenience, this geographical community can later gain a sustained competitive advantage because the richness of its network can lead to an environment that promotes advances and innovation (Jung, Kim, & Kim, 2019). Such advantages can range from reputation, to a social dislocation leading to accelerated uptake of the technology, to a dense network structure leading to quick diffusion of ideas, to an inflow of resources and capital investment.

Both the small world and Porter's lines of research integrate well with the arguments developed within the sociology of knowledge since the 1960s. Robert Merton (1972), Thomas Kuhn (1962), and Derek Price (1963) looked at the realm of science and research and argued that paradigms—lenses for viewing the world, frameworks of meaning—created tight clusters of researchers who built on each other's ideas. The stronger the paradigm, the more intellectually coordinated the cluster could be, since it had more clearly defined questions, methodologies, and language (Pfeffer, 1993; Yoels, 1974). On the other hand, maladjusted and restrictively strong paradigms can also lead to myopia, since higher commitment to a framework more strongly excludes other frameworks (Meyer & Zucker, 1989; Pfeffer, 1993).

Research within the scientific academy and within firms, traditionally studied separately, has begun to be more integrated as university researchers seek more patents, academic and corporate researchers fruitfully collaborate, and firms, such as Google, emerge from the ivory tower (Henderson, Jaffe, & Trajtenberg, 1998; Murray, 2005; Murray & Stern, 2005; Narin, Hamilton, & Olivastro, 1997; Shane, 2002). Nevertheless, studying fundamental and proprietary research separately is not completely unwarranted because the research settings rest on substantively distinct incentive structures (Gittelman & Kogut, 2003; Murray & Stern, 2005). Fundamental science encourages the broad distribution and sharing of knowledge, since the success of university researchers is bound-up with the attention of, and usefulness to, their fellow researchers. The importance of research within firms, while it builds on fundamental science (and sometimes contributes to it), rests on the ability to extract value from proprietary, and thus private, knowledge. These complementary uses of knowledge have encouraged flourishing knowledge communities that are a mix of public, academic, and private participants with derivative research conducted in tandem within firms to bring reified products to market, often conducted by the same researchers with a different emphasis. Researchers within firms are often vigorous, if sometimes conflicted, participants in their larger scientific communities (Gittelman & Kogut, 2003; Murray & Stern, 2005).

It is useful to look at the literature on "communities of practice," which argues that many core competencies of companies come from informal hands-on collaborative interaction, practice, observation, and learned know-how (Brown & Duguid, 1991, 2000; Wenger, 1998). Knowledge communities, while not contained by a formal organization, have the prerequisite qualities of repeated interaction, interdependency, norms, and learning to generate sustained core competencies built around shared methods, practices, capabilities, and routines (Brown & Duguid, 1991; Cohen, Nelson, & Walsh, 2000; Hwang, Singh, & Argote, 2015; Kolbjørnsrud, 2017; Lim & Ong, 2019; Sytch & Tatarynowicz, 2014).

Search

The search strategies used in research have been found to be very important to the nature and degree of the innovation that results from them. James March (1991) described two strategies firms can use when searching for new ideas or technologies. An *explorative search strategy* focuses on searching through unfamiliar material in the hope of a breakthrough that expands an area of specialty. An *exploitive search strategy* looks at areas of existing competence to find ways to better use or extract value from current resources.

Other studies have built on the importance of search scope in innovation. Nerkar (2003) studied whether firms that looked at old as well as recent technology had higher rates of innovation; while Gittelman (2003) examined whether geographic proximity to expertise increased technical know-how. Rosenkopf and Nerkar (2001) examined whether firms that looked at technology within or outside of their patent class, as well as within and outside their previous experience, were able to innovate more effectively. Katila and Ahuja (2002) argued for the efficacy of combining old and new technology for successful new product innovation.

A few generalizations about search patterns and innovation can be drawn from these studies. First, firms should explore somewhat widely when searching for new technology, though extreme or esoteric searches were sometimes found to be less fruitful. Second, flexibility in search patterns was advantageous; firms that only exploited existing or well-known resources did not, over time, perform well. Lastly, firms that looked for ideas in places where few others had looked, or who focused on still potent, unexhausted resources, tended to perform better.

Innovative performance is traditionally measured by focusing on patents, the firms' "claim" on a technology (Cohen et al., 2000; Pakes & Shankerman, 1984). Patents give their holders some rights over a certain piece of "intellectual property," and thereby incentivize firms to invest in R&D by allowing them to extract value from discoveries (Trajtenberg, 1990). Patents may be filed for other reasons, such as to block competitors; or firms can delay or purposely not file for patents in order to keep information on a discovery proprietary (Cohen et al., 2000; Murray & Stern, 2005). Although they are publicly available, patents are not filed to disseminate knowledge.

Marketing

The well-known theory of "integrated marketing" holds that organizations that present a unified and clear message to customers are more likely to perform well (Phelps & Johnson, 1966; Schultz, Tannenbaum, & Lauterborn, 1994). Customers seek confirmation of value by looking for convergence of messages; a message repeated by many people or through many channels is more likely to be viewed as more memorable and believable. By portraying a consistent message over time, organizations can develop an identity that could potentially lead to better performance (Stuart & Kerr, 1999). This consistency and dependability in marketing messages is the essence of brand identity, one of the most robust findings in the marketing literature (Haynes, Lackman, & Guskey, 1999).

A strongly focused, sharing, collaborative group culture can help gather and triangulate information about a market to maintain a better window into its needs and preferences (Hurley & Hult, 1998; Pfeffer, 1993; Powell, Kogut, & Smith-Doerr, 1996; Slater & Narver, 1995). Such a group has several interlocking abilities that allow it to communicate a message to the market in a unified, coherent way (Slater & Narver, 1995). The abilities to market products and ideas are not so different, as argued by literature on "science wars" and discussions on how ideas propagate as "memes" (Kogut & Macpherson, 2004). Strategies for selling ideas can be, in many ways, analogous to strategies for selling tangible products (Downs, 1957; Hotelling, 1929). Knowledge communities are interesting in this respect because the "market" for a knowledge community is primarily within the community and then secondarily—but necessarily—beyond the community. This increases the value of a shared internal form of presentation and uniform norms for use of language and methods (McCloskey, 1998).

It requires a shift in perspective to look at informal knowledge communities—something intangible that transcends formal organizations—instead of firms, geographies, or institutions. Looking at how these communities can communicate, change, and grow helps to make such a project less foreign. Much of the existing literature on search and marketing can be applied to knowledge communities to help understand how and why they are so fundamental to innovation.

HYPOTHESES

To take knowledge communities seriously requires we understand how they function, and that we understand, or try to understand, what makes them more or less successful. Here we build on our analysis to make specific predictions on what makes some knowledge communities more or less successful. For example, we believe that a knowledge community's use of *previous knowledge* will be closely related to the way it has searched its relevant knowledge-space for new ideas (Katila & Ahuja, 2002; Leahey, Beckman, & Stanko, 2017; Nerkar, 2003; Rosenkopf & Nerkar, 2001; Tortoriello, McEvily, & Krackhardt, 2015). On the other hand, we believe that a knowledge community's use of *language* will be more closely related to how it communicates internally and externally—how it markets its ideas to attract attention and members (Abrahamson, 1996; Piazza & Abrahamson, 2020; Powell et al., 1996; Slater & Narver, 1995). In both cases, we draw conceptually on the literature about paradigms and schools of thought for our unit of analysis (Crane, 1989; Kuhn, 1962). In explaining differential success, we believe that the existence and stability of community attributes, and their low appropriability, is best explained under a broad resource-based view framework that takes into account interconnected capabilities, norms, and routines.

Previous research has shown the importance to innovativeness of how a knowledge community searches for new ideas (Katila, 2002; Katila & Ahuja, 2002; Rosenkopf & Nerkar, 2001). The innovativeness of a knowledge community is at the very heart of its value, since it is composed of a cohesive collection of innovating researchers. Each researcher examines certain sources for good ideas, listing the useful ones as citations. Each researcher then contributes the results of this search, along with the good ideas that emerged during the process, as a paper or conference presentation. Others in the community, each doing his or her own research, can learn from and build on these ideas.

The information a knowledge community examines, therefore, will be determined by the aggregate of the resources its members examine. In the study of firms and patent citations, the aggregate citation pattern gives insight into the kind of search strategy used (Rosenkopf & Nerkar, 2001). Literature on search strategies implies that a broad search will be more likely to result in innovation (Cohen & Levinthal, 1990; Fleming, 2001; Fleming, Mingo, & Chen, 2005; Jung et al., 2019; March, 1991). Therefore, we believe that a firm that looks broadly at its intellectual landscape will be more likely to identify valuable sources of ideas. Understanding how and why knowledge communities create a culture of innovation that effectively generates and distributes good ideas is our central goal.

Hypothesis 1: Innovating knowledge communities that draw from diverse sources of knowledge will perform better.

A broad search, however, will only be useful to the extent that a knowledge community can exploit the good ideas it finds (March, 1991). In quickly moving areas of science, therefore, this ability to draw from sources with valuable ideas will be apparent in a knowledge community's ability to redirect its focus as an intellectual community as its research evolves and new areas of knowledge become more useful (Fleming, 2001; Levinthal & March, 1981).

The flexibility and speed with which a knowledge community can change to take advantage of opportunities will constitute an intellectual nimbleness that complements Hypothesis 1 (Fleming & Sorenson, 2001). In other words, the broad range of knowledge collected within a tight and interconnected knowledge community, as hypothesized above, allows such a community to scan the intellectual and technical landscape quickly and efficiently (Uzzi & Spiro, 2005; Watts, 1999). Coordination in a knowledge community requires quick diffusion of knowledge, since there is no formal hierarchical control. The ability to search broadly within a tight community and beyond it is crucial to finding valuable resources, and the ability to then reposition to take advantage of these resources is also crucial (Fleming & Sorenson, 2001; Rosenkopf & Nerkar, 2001).

Hypothesis 2: Innovating knowledge communities that are flexible in their use of knowledge will perform better.

It is important, as this chapter and other researchers have argued, for a firm to search and take advantage not only of standard resources but also of non-standard ones (Katila, 2003; Katila & Ahuja, 2002). Particularly where academia and industry mix, the emphasis is on ideas that contribute something innovative (Gittelman & Kogut, 2003; Henderson et al., 1998; Murray & Stern, 2005; Pakes & Shankerman, 1984).

Therefore, a knowledge community must not only search broadly and be flexible in its use of past knowledge, but it must also search in areas that are somewhat unique (Cohen & Levinthal, 1990; Drucker, 1985; Katila, 2003; Schumpeter, 1934). Ceteris paribus, the more competitors searching in an area, the less likely it is that undiscovered value can be found there (Porter, 1985). Further, it follows that a firm that searches broadly (hypothesis 1) and is flexible (hypothesis 2) will more likely be among the first to find valuable untapped resources, moving on by the time other, slower knowledge communities focus on these resources (Lieberman & Montgomery, 1988; Makadok, 1998).

Hypothesis 3: Knowledge communities that use unique knowledge will perform better.

Now we turn from the way knowledge communities use knowledge to the way they use, in aggregate, rhetoric. Knowledge communities in modern science and technology are largely text-based—that is, the primary form of communication between members is through articles. Knowledge communities have a particularly difficult signaling problem: Members need to identify each other in order to learn from each other and benefit from the advantages of community membership, but such identification is not always easy (Braam et al., 1991a, 1991b; White, 2003). Articles written by members of a knowledge community are part of that school only if a reader recognizes them as such—and community boundaries are vague and potentially overlapping. Since articles do not contain explicit school of thought identity labels (though journals can give hints toward potential identities), authors who wish to position their articles within a school may use keywords to identify themselves or may use language specific to that school (Abrahamson, 1996; McCloskey, 1998). The benefits of belonging to a school include a built-in audience, access to funding, and membership in a collaborative community (Kuhn, 1962).

From a marketing perspective, we expect rhetoric to be used in a knowledge community very differently from the way previous knowledge is used in a community. Members of strong knowledge communities will, we believe, for internal and external reasons, tend to converge on shared language both as a way to reduce the ambiguity of communication and because such communities use similar methodologies and similar language in presenting problems and issues (Abrahamson, 1996; Bartel & Saavedra, 2000; DiMaggio & Powell, 1983; McCloskey, 1998). As Lodahl and Gordon (1972) argue, "the high consensus found in high paradigm fields … provides an accepted and shared vocabulary for discussing the contents of the field" (p. 61). Further, according to Pfeffer (1993), "fields with highly developed paradigms, in which there is more consensus, should be characterized by more efficient communication—less time needed to be spent defining terms or explaining concepts … a high degree of consensus also makes interdependent activity more possible" (p. 601).

From an external perspective, literature on integrated marketing and branding suggests that firms that use a single consistent message will be more effective (Schultz et al., 1994). This should hold even more strongly for knowledge communities, where the lack of concrete labels causes authors to flag themselves as part of a school as a signaling message (Mizruchi & Fein, 1999; Pfeffer, 1993).

Lastly, the very diversity of knowledge being presented by knowledge communities gives rise to a need for a single rhetorical lens with which to express these ideas. Literature on paradigms suggests they are a way of looking at the world—a framework for analysis. Successful knowledge communities, we believe, will draw on many sources for their knowledge and then present these diverse ideas under one shared rhetoric or framework of analysis.

Hypothesis 4: Innovating knowledge communities that use consistent rhetoric will perform better.

The lack of formal leadership that makes knowledge communities so different from firms also limits their ability to coordinate change. The rhetoric of a strong paradigm tends to be stable over time, as it is based on a shared construction of rhetorical meaning (Price, 1963). Reconceptualizations of shared mental constructions and changes in meaning of shared language, particularly in a context without any explicit leadership or coordinating mechanism, are difficult and confusing, and can result in inefficiency and ambiguity in communication. Indeed, radical shifts in language often signal a paradigm shift where one knowledge community supplants another.

The advantages of shifting rhetoric over time are not as clear. Buzzwords and rhetorical fashion are not a good basis for a sustained competitive advantage, particularly in a field that relies on technical work (Abrahamson, 1996; Piazza & Abrahamson, 2020). Since knowledge communities are amorphous groups without formal boundaries, they benefit from a unified use of language in order to create a recognizable identity or brand (Haynes et al., 1999). Particularly in a technical context, language is not the source of innovation; rather, the ideas underlying language are. Therefore, once a knowledge community constructs a consensus in rhetoric, it remains relatively stable.

Hypothesis 5: Innovating knowledge communities that use stable rhetoric will perform better.

Finally, knowledge communities, if they are to be successful, must appeal to large numbers of people. This implies that schools claim and use common and recognized language as their core set of words, allowing them to grab the metaphorical "middle ground" (Downs, 1957; Hotelling, 1929). Knowledge communities, whose words and meanings are difficult for others to understand, tend to isolate themselves. While this has proven to be a successful strategy for professional fields that desire barriers to entry (e.g., medicine and law), it hampers the cooperation and collaboration that is desirable between knowledge communities (Kripke, 1982). Scientists in separate knowledge communities within a field, particularly technical fields with interdependent technologies, and with mobility between fields, would find it a disadvantage to isolate a field rhetorically. Addressing the important issues of the field and communicating good ideas in broadly understood language will lead to the largest possible audience (Downs, 1957).

Hypothesis 6: Innovating knowledge communities that use mainstream rhetoric will perform better.

Although knowledge communities do not have formal leaders or formal organizational legitimacy, they do have the preconditions for idiosyncratic capabilities and routines—intense socialization, repeated interactions, mechanisms for punishment and reward, an interconnected incentive structure (Barney, Wright, & Ketchen, 2001; Cohen et al., 2000; Wernerfelt, 1984). These differential routines and capabilities could constitute a competitive advantage for communities and lead some communities to have sustained levels of higher innovativeness.

The effect of firm involvement in knowledge communities is interesting. While it is not a main variable, we include it in order to explore its impact on all our models. One chief difference between firms and the knowledge communities we present in this work is that firms place a higher value on proprietary information. A firm may have a strong incentive to keep valuable knowledge internal and unshared, and it may also have the central coordination and legal sanctions to do so (non-disclosure agreements, threat of termination, loyalty to group, etc.). Knowledge communities, on the other hand, often thrive on open information sharing, at least in the sciences and social sciences. The difference this makes is hard to fully appreciate until our analysis extends to firms or commercial patents.

We chose to do our analysis in a context where knowledge communities were arguably the dominant group-level organizing principle. This allowed us to better isolate the impact of this form of organizational structure on innovation and knowledge development. Extending this analysis should be increasingly useful the more clearly we can establish its elements. The promise already exists; Gerlach (1992), for example, conducted a clustering analysis on firms in Japan and found that the technique placed firms in meaningful networks.

We believe that firm involvement should increase in promising knowledge communities because firms try to become involved with knowledge communities they perceive as having meaningful breakthroughs, and their involvement may, in turn, give the community additional resources. The causal direction of this link—whether firm involvement increases knowledge community success through additional resources or whether it is a consequence of community success—is very difficult to test empirically.

By posing hypotheses that can be proved or disproved by our data, we are testing the validity of our intellectual framework in knowledge communities. If we are identifying something intellectually and scientifically/technologically real, then we believe we will be able to get significant results. Thinking about the world in terms of knowledge communities allows us to ask a set of questions and predict a set of cluster-level behaviors that would not be meaningful or possible when looked at from the perspective of a corporation, geography or institution. We hope this will give us additional insight into how science and technology evolve and develop.

METHODS AND DATA

While theory on knowledge communities is useful, too often when we study things "in the wild," they function very differently. We chart how knowledge communities function in the real world in order to see how the innovators interact within and between formal organizations to create new knowledge. Such an exploration requires a very granular look into one area, preferably an area of interest and importance to technology, where insight can be useful and relevant. If we can do this, then we can potentially better understand how and why some areas of technology accelerate so rapidly and why some do not.

We chose computer science as our area of study. We did this partly because so many recent technological breakthroughs have been in the world of bytes, and partly because it is much more dynamic and fast-moving than many other areas of science. This allowed us to study innovation and clusters in a dynamic and important context. The data in this chapter were drawn largely from CiteSeer, a digital library of papers from conferences and journals in computer science. CiteSeer collects computer science papers posted on the Internet by linking directly to publishers, conference sites, and journals, and then parses these articles to find the citations and descriptive information in each paper.

Computer science is a quickly evolving industry that has a historical preference for open disclosure of information, despite proprietary value, as the practice of open sourcing and the popularity of Linux among computer scientists illustrates. It is common practice, therefore, to place most papers on freely available author, conference, and publisher websites, and virtually all computer scientists have the resources and expertise to do this. As a consequence, CiteSeer has a large collection of over 700,000 indexed papers in its database. We cross-referenced all of these papers with the DBLP Computer Science Bibliography, a European database with over 600,000 papers that indexes a similar group of computer science papers, in order to verify existing information and gather supplemental information on journals and conferences. The match between these two databases was close; indeed, the DBLP links most of its papers to the corresponding papers in the CiteSeer database.

The majority of papers in these databases are from between 1992 and 2003. Earlier papers preceded the Internet's common use for posting papers, even among early adopters in the computer science community, and more recent papers are still being posted or are still under review for publication. These databases give us a rich picture of the field of computer science as it evolved during this period.

Clustering Methodology

That knowledge communities exist is one thing, but measuring them over time is actually quite hard. One problem is that the field is dynamic, and so findings can be unstable year-on-year. Another is that knowledge communities in the real world can merge, split, emerge, and die. This instability and dynamism introduces complexity when measuring knowledge communities/clusters over time. To find our knowledge communities, we used a clustering algorithm to identify clusters of like papers. Our methodology utilized the structure of co-citations in paper bibliographies to group papers that are "similar" in the papers they cite, representing the similar knowledge they are building on (Small & Sweeney, 1985). Essentially, therefore, we compared the citations of all papers to all other papers, to find papers that use similar citations. We believe that a fundamental aspect of these knowledge communities is the interplay and sequential contribution of work as computer scientists learn from and build on each other's work (Ma & Uzzi, 2018; Niemann, Moehrle, & Frischkorn, 2017; Small, 2018a).

When previous research in management and innovation has used algorithms for clustering, two methods have been overwhelmingly prevalent: CONCOR and hierarchical clustering. CONCOR has been used to cluster patterns of employee coopetition within firms, firms based on alliances, and intercorporate relationships in Japan (Gerlach, 1992; Hagedoorn & Duysters, 2002; Tsai, 2002). Hierarchical clustering, on the other hand, is more intuitively understandable because it compares all agents (in our case, computer science researchers) to each other and systematically merges them until told to stop. Nohria and Garcia-Pont (1991) used hierarchical clustering to compare two firm organizing principles—firm capabilities and firm alliances—and checked their clustering results with the alternative methodology, kmeans. These methods work best in smaller datasets with low dimensionality and clear cluster divisions. Their chief weakness, as with other ad hoc, single-pass methods in management (Aharonson et al., 2004), is that their initial clustering choices result in path dependency. That is, once CONCOR splits a dataset, that division is never reevaluated (and, indeed, with this methodology, cannot be) after later splits. Similarly, once a hierarchical clustering program has merged two agents or groups of agents, that merge is never reevaluated after future merges. But subsequent evaluation of group similarities may suggest a repartitioning of data that is incompatible with previous path-dependent partitioning choices. As datasets grow larger and are specified with higher dimensions, and clusters become more nuanced, these methods become increasingly flawed.

In some technical and scientific areas, particularly Internet search and bioinformatics, which have to analyze enormous databases, more advanced techniques have been developed. These methods take advantage of exponentially greater computational power to make multiple passes over the data—minimizing the effect of clustering path dependency and allowing for accurate clustering of much larger multi-dimensional databases (Kandylas, 2005; Pantel & Lin, 2002; Popescul et al., 2000).

To study knowledge communities, we needed a method with some demanding requirements. We wanted a clustering methodology that was explicitly dynamic—which allowed for clusters to emerge and disappear—and that was strictly backward-looking (i.e., did not allow subsequent events to impact clustering patterns or distance measures from earlier in the time range). This backward-looking and dynamic perspective is relevant when looking at the research landscapes from the perspective of a particular researcher at a particular point in time. Further, we wanted to allow a substantial proportion of our data to not be in a cluster at all. We believe that the delicate relationships that form knowledge communities are not ubiquitous or necessary for research—though they are not uncommon. Lastly, the size and complexity of our database required a program that could handle large and high-dimensional datasets as elegantly and efficiently as possible.

Therefore, to identify knowledge communities we built on prior clustering methodologies to develop a new clustering approach, StrEMer, that produces high-quality clusters that are dynamic over time and allows papers that are not tightly connected to a cohesive set of research to remain out of a cluster (Kandylas, 2005; Zhong & Ghosh, 2003). Inspired by the Clustering By Committee (CBC) algorithm, our algorithm uses typical cluster features, as opposed to using the average of all cluster elements or a single representative element, to define its elements. The three-step methodology reduced path dependency dramatically, since the steps are completed simultaneously and dynamically. We used streaming clustering to form many seed clusters; evaluate the seed clusters in terms of tightness and minimum size threshold, with the best committees designated as clusters and the rest discarded; and assigned specific elements to the nearest committee or exclude them from all committees.

Our algorithm constructs a similarity measure using a "feature vector" for each element to represent the citation patterns between this element and other elements. We then computed the similarity between two elements A and B (hypothetically illustrated in Figure 2.1) using the cosine coefficient of their feature vectors:

$$\cos(v) = sim(A, B) = \frac{\sum\limits_{k} A_k \cdot B_k}{\sqrt{\sum\limits_{k} A_k^2 \cdot \sum\limits_{k} B_k^2}}$$

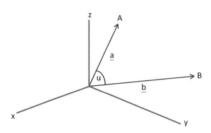

Figure 2.1   Visualization of a cluster using vector angles to represent paper similarity in high dimensional space

We further defined the similarity between an element e and a cluster c as the similarity between e and the cluster feature centroid of c: $sim(e,c)=sim(e,cen)$, where cen is the cluster feature centroid vector of c. Finally, the similarity between two clusters c_i and c_j is the similarity between their cluster feature centroid vectors: $sim(c_i, c_j)=sim(cen_i, cen_j)$, where cen_i and cen_j are centroid vectors of c_i and c_j respectively.

In Figure 2.2, w and x represent groups of papers that will become clusters, while y and z represent lone papers that will not be assigned to clusters. In this simplified example, the papers appear as points on the circle, extending from a common starting point—the origin, where similar papers are very near each other on the circumference of the circle. Another way of measuring this "closeness" is to look at the angle between each pair of papers. Clusters are identified by our method by searching for groups of papers with small angles between them (in a high-dimensional space).

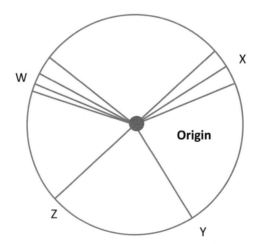

Note: Here, w and x represent groups of very similar papers, while y and z represent papers that are more different.

Figure 2.2   Similar papers in a cluster can be depicted as closer together (smaller vector angle)

All standard clustering methods create clusters based on citations made both by a paper and by other similar papers published subsequently, conflating the importance of a cluster in the future with its position now. But in reality, agents at any time point can only look backward in time to determine their intellectual landscapes.

We developed an iterative clustering scheme ("rolling clustering") that successfully resolved this temporal confounding. Our clustering algorithm looks only backward in time to determine clusters in a given year, and this process is then repeated for the next year before clusters from each analysis are "linked." An appropriate temporal overlap must be included to ensure consistency in cluster composition. Thus, we executed the rolling clustering using a five-year window: First, we ran the clustering algorithm on the data from the first five years, i.e., 1992–1996, recording the cluster assignments at the termination of the algorithm. Next, we again ran the clustering algorithm, this time using only the data from the next time period, i.e., 1993–1997. We then matched-up clusters over time using the overlapping years of the two clustering runs (in the case above, 1992–1996).

Figure 2.3 graphically displays a hypothetical series of rolls. Clusters A and C appear throughout the 3 rolls. Cluster B disappears in the third roll. Cluster D appears in the second roll. Throughout the rolls, the slow dynamic movement of the clusters as they change over time is visible. Essentially, we chained together a series of overlapping clusterings to create continuity while allowing for an evolving knowledge landscape.

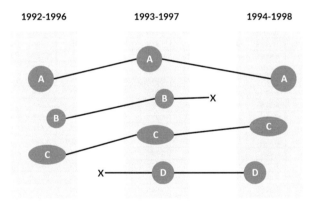

Note: Clusters linked across time periods (cluster A and cluster C). Existing clusters can disappear (cluster B), and new clusters can form (cluster D).

Figure 2.3   Hypothetical rolls and clusterings

This process allows all cluster assignments in each year to be backward-looking only, based on the previous five-year frame—an appropriate "context" for knowledge development. At the same time, we find very high continuity between clusters, since the knowledge landscape we created changes gradually. Another benefit of this method is that our measures of "centrality" at the paper and cluster levels refer to the appropriate frame rather than an aggregate over the entire time range, as with all other standard methods.

Identifying Innovating Communities

Unlike most previous clustering methods, our process allows us to dynamically track clusters over time. Further, the clusters observed in each year of our dataset are what agents looking at that intellectual landscape would see at that time (i.e., in real time without the benefits of hindsight). The evolution of clusters over time, therefore, can be seen as a result of the choices agents make as they, in aggregate, position themselves on this landscape. The evolution of the intellectual landscape, seen in Table 2.1, represents the evolution of computer science from 1992 to 2003. These years marked a dramatic growth of computer science and radical evolution of its scope of use. To further test the validity of our method, with common sense we ask: Do the knowledge communities we found accurately reflect and shed light on the changes in computer science during this period? Appendix 2.1 gives details on the 21 knowledge communities we identified. It provides graphs of the growth of each knowledge community over time, as well as a sense of each community's appearances and disappearances. It also details our proposed names for each knowledge community and provides some details (top three most cited papers, top keywords, etc.). Appendix 2.2 provides an MDS plot of how the communities relate to each other each year for both rhetoric and citation.

	1992	1993	1994	1995	1996	1997	1998	1999	2000	2001	2002	2003
1	9.23%	11.85%	10.76%	9.14%	7.06%	7.23%	7.42%	7.34%	6.58%	5.15%	4.57%	4.24%
2	15.85%	10.55%	11.93%	10.44%	7.52%	7.61%	7.70%	8.16%	8.44%	8.36%	7.58%	8.95%
3	7.84%	7.05%	8.38%	6.05%	6.06%	6.73%	5.91%	7.21%	6.22%	5.86%	4.48%	4.91%
4	7.49%	9.09%	5.46%	6.22%	5.84%	4.67%	5.25%	4.23%	1.85%			
5	4.01%	3.42%	7.65%	7.28%	8.92%	9.65%	9.19%	6.50%				
6	1.92%	2.55%	3.63%	3.59%	6.13%	6.33%	5.56%	5.58%	5.78%	6.02%	4.71%	3.70%
7	9.06%	10.76%	5.80%	4.66%	4.08%	3.30%	3.16%	3.29%	2.67%	3.18%	3.04%	2.89%
8	3.31%	3.71%	6.76%	7.21%	8.04%	8.25%	6.97%	6.58%	7.45%	6.63%	4.31%	5.32%
9	17.94%	17.02%	10.01%	8.58%	10.02%	8.02%	7.22%	8.11%	5.67%	7.33%	9.23%	5.85%
10	4.18%	6.91%	8.45%	10.32%	10.23%	9.37%	9.42%	10.29%	8.35%	8.03%	7.51%	5.11%
11	0.17%	0.36%	0.46%	2.15%	4.98%	5.77%	6.15%	6.68%	4.77%	5.85%	6.48%	6.53%
12			3.59%	5.57%	5.86%	7.82%	7.71%	5.30%	4.40%	4.02%	2.44%	
13			2.67%	5.35%	5.02%	5.86%	7.52%	9.59%	13.57%	12.08%	10.76%	10.90%
14	14.29%	12.36%	9.02%	8.76%	6.36%	3.91%	3.92%	1.82%	1.41%			
15	4.36%	2.18%	3.40%	2.45%	1.28%	1.18%	1.03%	0.35%				
16					0.04%	0.29%	0.50%	0.95%	3.91%	5.42%	7.08%	8.55%
17					0.29%	0.79%	1.23%	2.21%	3.97%	5.61%	6.87%	7.60%
18					0.23%	0.45%	0.90%	1.29%	4.32%	5.53%	5.96%	7.20%
19	0.35%	2.18%	2.01%	2.23%	0.51%	0.31%	0.28%	0.12%				
20					1.56%	2.46%	2.25%	2.77%	4.54%	4.56%	6.16%	7.74%
21							0.71%	1.63%	6.11%	6.35%	8.83%	10.50%

Notes: 1993–1994: Split of cluster 14 into cluster 14 (40%) and 12 (23%); 1995–1996: Split of cluster 9 into cluster 9 (38%) and 17 (16%); 1999–2000: Merge of cluster 6 and 15 into cluster 6; 2000–2001: Merge of cluster 12 and 14 into cluster 12 (see previous split).

Table 2.1   *Cluster size as percentage of total papers in knowledge communities over time*

In 1992, we observe 14 knowledge communities. Between 1992 and 1999, seven new knowledge communities formed and none disappeared. This finding is in keeping with the dramatic growth of computer science during the Internet boom in California's Silicon Valley and around the world. In these years, the Nasdaq, which is an index disproportionately heavy with technology and internet stocks, rose from approximately 600 to 4,000.

From 1999 to 2001, five knowledge communities disappeared and none were created. These broad cluster trends are in keeping with the collapse of the Internet bubble and the fall of the Nasdaq from 1999 to 2001 to almost 2,000. The movement and rates of change of clusters also reflect these changes, with more activity during times of shakeup in 2000 to 2001 as knowledge communities collectively struggle to readjust to and survive a period of dramatic correction in the sector. The general trends in our data examining computer science knowledge communities closely track changes in the financial sector.

The insights from literature on paradigm shifts and disruptive technologies can be seen in microcosm here. For example, clusters 5 and 21 represent very similar topics—"machine vision/graphics" and "image analysis/tracking," respectively—but are very distinct communities. In the mid-1990s, the first (cluster 5) experienced a steep decline as a research community, while the latter cluster emerged from nowhere and became quite significant. Clusters 4 and 20 on "design of cryptographic systems" and "cryptography," respectively, experienced the same pattern, with cluster 20 seeming to emerge and grab cluster 4's intellectual space. These seem to be examples of established communities of researchers being unable to absorb or compete with emerging research communities. These sorts of "disruptive shifts" or "paradigm shifts" are addressed in the literature in technology and the sociology of knowledge (Henderson & Clark, 1990; Kuhn, 1962). During the mid-1990s, as the Internet grew exponentially and broadband allowed video to be more easily transferred and stored, we also saw the emergence of two clusters on "congestion control" and "image analysis/tracking." At the same time, we saw the decline of "distributed computing" and "shared memory/parallel processing." These trends seem to fit the intuitive understanding of trends in computer science and were strongly confirmed by computer scientists examining these results.

Other clusters merge and split, potentially representing a schism of a knowledge community or the absorption of one knowledge community by another. Our dynamic clustering methodology allows some insight into how knowledge evolves and changes. For example, between 1993 and 1994, cluster 14, representing the knowledge community studying "shared memory/ parallel processing," split, forming cluster 12, a new cluster focusing on "parallel computing." In terms of size, 40% of the papers from cluster 14 remained, and 23% split off, resulting in two smaller clusters. This trend continued, with cluster 12 growing faster than cluster 14, until 2001, when they merged to form one cluster again. In effect, a knowledge community split into two, and the new group was successful enough to eventually absorb the group from which it originally split (Figure 2.4).

In 1996, cluster 9, representing the knowledge community researching "Internet traffic management", shattered to form several smaller clusters. Most fragments were below the threshold of size and cohesiveness to be knowledge communities, consisting of a few loosely related papers, but there did remain remnants of the original cluster, 9, and a new cluster, 17, which represented "distributed computing." Both were significantly smaller—at 38% and 16%, respectively, of the size of the original cluster 9 (Figure 2.5).

In 2000, there was also a merger between clusters 6 and 15, representing the knowledge communities researching "constraint satisfaction" and "optimization," respectively. These fields are clearly related, and both clusters were approximately the same size. Cluster 15 was on the tail end of a gradual decline, and cluster 6 was recently formed and consistently growing, so we labeled the resulting knowledge community as cluster 6 (Figure 2.6).

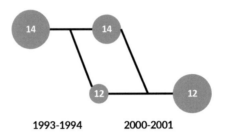

Figure 2.4   Clusters split and merge

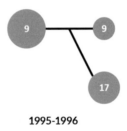

Figure 2.5   Clusters split

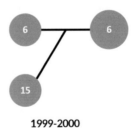

Figure 2.6   Clusters merge

We also saw the emergence of a number of clusters that were not present at the start of our study. In 1996, a new cluster emerged on "Internet search." One of its top three most cited papers is by Larry Page and Sergey Brin, the founders of Google, who built their first search engine in 1996, founded a company in 1998, and went on to have a multi-billion-dollar IPO in 2004. In 1996, the knowledge community representing "Internet search" comprised only 0.23% of our computer science papers—in 2003, it represents 7.20%. This leads to a compound annual growth rate (CAGR) of 51.74% from 1998, when Google was founded, to 2003—the second highest of all clusters, after only cluster 16, representing the related topic of "congestion control," which also emerged in 1996.

We do not believe the rise and fall of these fields was determined by exogenous macro trends in technology, though they do confirm them. Indeed, computer science changes so quickly that it seems to evolve to some extent according to what is technically possible rather than what is explicitly demanded—potential uses emerge, and users find them useful (though one could argue there is latent demand). Academic, not proprietary, research in computer science defines the boundaries of the field, and many advances begin here before spilling out into firms (Henderson et al., 1998). This implies that, to some significant extent, it is the discoveries and creativity of knowledge communities that shape the evolution of computer science, making them an even more significant area of study. Computer scientists we showed this clustering to were particularly interested in the emerging trends our method may be able to predict or clarify—what clusters are emerging and growing in the future. This methodology may be able to give us insight into not only what happened historically, but what will happen going forward in an area of research (Table 2.2).

We extended our analysis by seeing if we could begin to define the attributes of knowledge communities that lead to their differential success.

Attributes of Knowledge Communities

What attributes influence the creativity and success of a knowledge community? We believe we can identify a number of relevant and powerful variables for analysis at the cluster level. Looking at clusters, we can ask questions that previous researchers could not isolate meaningfully—in particular, strategic (i.e., outcome-oriented) questions whose answers can help us understand and accelerate innovation.

Performance Variables: Our dependent variable for cluster was a measure of the "vigor", or performance, of a cluster at a given time. To model this, we used the number of papers presented at conferences or published in computer science journals in a cluster from 1992 to 2003, controlling for the number of papers published the year before. Thus, effectively, we measured the performance of an intellectual community controlling for the prior year's number of papers published.

To generate this variable, we aggregated number of papers published by each cluster into year-long time periods, consistent with a broad set of network papers in technology and strategy (Rosenkopf & Nerkar, 2001). This provided us with a summary measure of how many "members" an intellectual community was able to both attract and promote. To simplify the relative scale of our data, we divided the number of papers by 1,000 in our regressions.

Table 2.2   *Summary statistics for clusters*

Cluster #	Total Papers	Total Cites	Cite/Paper	InClustBib	CAGR
1	7892	50924	6.45	44.29%	−6.83%
2	9368	70414	7.52	41.04%	−5.06%
3	7022	46199	6.58	42.92%	−4.16%
4	4144	39962	9.64	28.39%	n/a
5	6053	50990	8.42	22.74%	n/a
6	6070	39854	6.57	37.53%	6.17%
7	3968	32076	8.08	38.23%	−9.85%
8	7743	47861	6.18	38.94%	4.40%
9	9002	89961	9.99	27.49%	−9.68%
10	10180	86158	8.46	40.72%	1.85%
11	5890	52377	8.89	28.85%	39.01%
12	5990	32899	5.49	43.11%	−13.59%
13	9566	52569	5.50	41.58%	13.82%
14	3818	39589	10.37	26.85%	n/a
15	950	7050	7.42	14.18%	n/a
16	2297	12239	5.33	24.03%	76.57%
17	2743	15890	5.79	23.37%	44.07%
18	2428	12307	5.07	29.32%	51.74%
19	472	3886	8.23	10.24%	n/a
20	3289	26104	7.94	32.88%	28.04%
21	3043	11185	3.68	18.51%	11.44%

Notes: Variables represent totals for clusters from 1992 to 2003, or from emergence to disappearance from data. Cite/Paper is the average citations received by a paper in that cluster.
InClustBib is calculated as the % of citations made by a cluster to papers also in that cluster. CAGR of clusters that emerge during data range are calculated beginning their second year in data.

Cohesiveness: We were interested in seeing if the intellectual "cohesiveness" or "overlap" of both the shared rhetoric (words) and shared knowledge (papers cited) of the knowledge community are significant for predicting its performance. Our goal was to find a measure of how paradigmatic knowledge and language are within a school of thought.

For the *Knowledge Cohesiveness* variable, we represented how widely the cluster as a whole searched for knowledge during that year in the intellectual landscape vs. how focused (coordinated) that search was. This was done by computing the average similarity between the citations structure of each paper and the overall citations structure of the cluster, where similarity is as defined in the previous clustering period. Building on our previous illustration in the clustering description, we plotted a vector for the citations of each paper in a cluster and compared each line to the average line for that cluster.

We constructed a similar variable for rhetoric in the cluster by taking the title and keywords of each paper and, as is common, removing "stop" words, such as "and," "if," and "by", and then "stemming" them so that, for example, Learning and Artificial Intelligence becomes Learn Artifici Intellig. We then constructed the *Rhetorical Cohesiveness* variable as we constructed *Knowledge Cohesiveness* above. This is a proxy for how similarly people in a cluster use language.

The average of these for each cluster in each year is a measure of the extent to which a cluster's use of rhetoric is narrow or disperse, and the extent to which a cluster's use of knowledge is focused or expansive. This is measured as:

$$\frac{\sum_{i=1}^{n_c} sim(e_i, cen_c)}{n_c}$$

where C represents a cluster for a given year; i indexes papers in cluster C, and nC is the number of papers in cluster C; and $sim(\cdot)$ is the measure of similarity as previously defined in the clustering methodology. These processes yield measures, relative to other clusters, of how dispersed or focused the use of knowledge and the use of rhetoric are for this cluster in this year.

Uniqueness: We were also interested in how different an intellectual community is, either in the knowledge it generates or in the rhetoric it uses, from other intellectual communities. *Uniqueness of Rhetoric* represents how unique the rhetoric of a school of thought is at a given point in time compared to other clusters. A school of thought that is very unique/not unique uses, on aggregate, language that is substantively different from/similar to the words and word combinations in other schools of thought. *Uniqueness of Knowledge* is a measure that represents how unique the sources of knowledge of a school of thought are at a given point in time. A school of thought that has a distinctive citation structure has derived its knowledge from sources that are very different from those used by other schools of thought. The variable is computed in the same way as *Uniqueness of Rhetoric*, using citation structure rather than words.

In this calculation, we focused on the average citation or rhetoric for a cluster, and compared it to all other clusters' average citations or rhetoric. For example, if a cluster generally uses the same keywords or cites the same papers, the average for this cluster will be small.

Rate of Change: Adaptability or rate of change for a cluster is an important measure of how flexible it is over time. We were interested in the tendencies of a cluster to change or remain stable. We assumed that over time in a changing environment, flexible clusters move more than less flexible clusters. Since knowledge changes as a function of other knowledge, we used a relative measure of change in constructing this variable. Given the averages or centroids for citation structure and language per cluster, we constructed a cosine similarity between each cluster and itself in the previous year. The difference between the cluster average from year t to $t+1$ is a measure of the "rate of change" of a cluster over time. To smooth out this number over time, we take the three-year running average as our variable of interest. However, a cluster's average rates of change over 1, 2, 5, and all years were comparable. The change in rhetoric represents how much the words a cluster uses change (operationalized, as described previously) from one year to the next; the change in knowledge represents how much a cluster's average use of citations (or the knowledge sources it draws from) changes from one year to the next. It is defined as:

$$\frac{\sum_{t=0}^{T} sim(cen_{T-t}, cen_{T-(t+1)})}{T}$$

where t indexes the years considered in the formula; T is the span of years we consider; and $sim(\cdot)$ is the measure of similarity, as previously defined.

Controls

Leadership Controls: A common way to explain differential performance in firms is to look at the level of leadership or coordination. It is not clear in informal knowledge communities what leadership means or whether leadership is significant. To attempt to measure leadership in knowledge communities, we tested for the effects of leadership (or coordination) on three levels—from members of the community, for concentration of the institutions the members identify with, and for concentration in distribution in the community (Porter, 1998).

While an intellectual community does not have CEOs or boards, it may have very influential members who can act as intellectual leaders, coordinating the knowledge community's chief concerns, methodologies, and areas of research (Pfeffer, 1993). We identified influence ties between authors of papers and the authors of the papers they cited, and thereby construct an influence network for each cluster. We then ran centrality measures on these networks to measure the clusters' eigenvector, degree, and in-degree centrality. We found eigenvector to be the most useful measure of centrality, since it measures both direct and indirect influence, though all measures led to similar results (see robustness, Table 2.5).

We also controlled for the potential coordinating influence of institutions. For example, a school, such as MIT, or a company, such as Google, might be home to a significant number of members of a school of thought, and thus the formal control, social network, institutional norms, and institutional organization these institutions exhibit may contribute to the de facto coordination of the school of thought. To construct a variable to measure this, we first identified the institutions that the authors in the database identified within their papers. We then found the percentage of papers for each cluster that came from the most common 10 schools, research institutions, or companies to see if a cluster had concentrated influences to a few institutions. We also measured the concentration of the top 1, 2, 3, and 5 institutions and received similar results. We assumed that a higher concentration of control by a few players in a knowledge cluster increases the potential for cluster coordination.

Lastly, we feel a coordinating or leadership role might be played if an intellectual community is dominated by a powerful institution that controls distribution for that cluster—such as a journal or conference that acts as a gatekeeper for the community. Such knowledge gatekeepers can implicitly or explicitly influence the level of homogeneity and coordination of a school of thought by both lending legitimacy to work (by certifying it has passed a rigorous review process) and making it available to an interested audience. In this case, we looked at the percentage of articles published in the 10 most common venues of the authors (either journals or conferences).

Prestige Controls: Prestige is a powerful factor in explaining differential performance in organizations; we wished to test whether this also holds true for knowledge communities. As with leadership, we therefore controlled for prestige on the member, journal/conference, and employer/university levels of analysis. For members, we wish to control for the prestige that would result from the "top" members of a field preferring to publish in some intellectual communities, leading to superior performance. We constructed this variable by finding the authors who had been nominated to the prestigious post of fellow by three top societies in computer science—the Institute for Electrical and Electronics Engineers, the Association of Computing Machinery, and the National Academy of Engineering, from 1975 to 2005, and counting the number of these fellows who published in any of our intellectual communities by cluster and year. Next, we constructed a variable that counted the number of papers coming from the most prestigious 20 universities in computer science, as ranked by the US News and World Report graduate school rankings of academic programs. By doing this, we helped control for the tendency of some intellectual communities to be associated with prestigious institutions. Lastly, we constructed a variable that counted the number of papers published in the top 10 most prestigious journals, as ranked by impact factor in Thomson ISI's Impact Factors, and the top 10 most prestigious conferences, as ranked by citation impact by DBLP. We took these counts broken-up by cluster and by year, and ranked them within year by cluster. This rank-ordered list of clusters by year indicated the relative prestige of knowledge communities on multiple levels.

Industry/Academia Controls: Each author of each paper was coded as being affiliated with a firm or academic/research institution. We then coded each paper as "academic" if all of its authors were affiliated with academic/research institutions, "industry" if all of its authors had firm affiliations, and "mixed" if some of its authors were affiliated with firms and some with academic/research institutions. We entered this information into the regression by including the three categorical variables "mixed", "academic" and "industry."

Previous thinking about schools of thought and knowledge building has seldom quantified and tested it. We attempted here, however imperfectly, to not only speak of how such knowledge building might work but to use our clustering methodology to identify these knowledge communities. We used theory developed in the strategic and academic literature to make concrete predictions on how such clusters might behave.

KNOWLEDGE COMMUNITIES IN THE REAL WORLD

With a concrete dataset in computer science, and key questions and variables defined, the question can finally be answered: Does analysis at the knowledge community level result in meaningful and coherent insights? If such clusters are coherent but meaningless (say, the first letter of the authors' last names), analysis would yield little or no meaningful differences in outcomes or performance (and no intuitive meaning). Here we take our previous insights and test them using statistical analysis. Since our data encompassed dynamic communities and measured their characteristics over time, we used a cross-sectional time series model to gain insight into the effects of community attributes. We estimated our models using Generalized Least Squares (GLS), including robust standard errors for determining statistical significance.

This approach allowed us to investigate the time trends within our data while also adjusting our standard errors for intragroup correlations. This was necessary because we believed the performance measures of any cluster would be correlated over time. In addition, we evaluated a variety of plausible model estimation methods, chiefly a Generalized Estimating Equations (GEE) approach, an explicit panel-data GLS model, and a Random Effects specification, estimated via maximum likelihood, all of which are explored further in our robustness section.

A Wooldridge test for first-order autocorrelation in panel data (Drukker, 2003; Wooldridge, 2002) found that, as expected, our data exhibited autocorrelation, which implies that a time lag will be required to ensure independence of residuals ($F_{(1,21)}$ = 228.358, p < 0.0001). After testing different lag periods for appropriateness using Akaike's Information Criterion (AIC), we included the cluster's prior year performance in the model (one-year lag) as a predictor.

Our dependent variable was a measure of the performance of the intellectual community over time. Since our dataset consisted of papers published in the field of computer science from 1992 to 2003, we chose to use the total number of papers published by each community in each given calendar year as a measure of cluster vigor or "success." We included a one-year lag in the regression as well, controlling for the prior size of the cluster one year earlier.

The empirical goal of our model was to explore the extent to which we can measure community attributes and use them to predict performance. The central question we faced was how the community uses rhetoric and draws on knowledge, both of which are unrelated to the verisimilitude or explanatory power of the community, to enable it to be successful. Specifically, we considered how the community draws on past knowledge and generates persuasive rhetoric by measuring the cohesiveness and uniqueness of both. We estimated our model as follows:

$$y_{it} = \beta \cdot x_{it} + b_i \cdot z_{it} + e_{it}$$

where i indexes clusters from 1 to n, t indexes years (time), and (1) y_{it} denotes the response variable, (2) β represents the portion of effects that is constant across clusters (the fixed effects), (3) b_i represents the portion of our effects that varies between individuals (the random effects), (4) x_{it} is the vector of our predictors, (5) z_{it} is a subset of our predictors x_{it}, and (6) e_{it} represents the error term for our model.

Our base assumption was that our response was multivariate-normally distributed: $Y \sim MVN[\beta X, V]$, where V is a block diagonal, symmetric, matrix as $V = \text{diag}[V1, V2, \ldots, Vn]$ with each component matrix Vi composed of two components: $V_i = \Sigma_{zi} + T_{zi}$.

In our chosen specification, Σ_{zj} signifies the usual error terms arising from the random effects model, while T_{zj} is an optional additional term that reflects the alternative error possibilities we explore later in our robustness section. For our chosen models we have simply $V_i = \Sigma_i$.

Models

We arrived at our full model by analyzing variables systematically to examine their marginal effects as well as the end joint effects. Model I contained only the control variables—leadership, prestige, and the industry/academic dummy variables. In Models II through IV, we considered first our variables for community cohesiveness, then our variables for community uniqueness, and lastly our variables for community flexibility. Finally, in Model V, we considered our full model with all community attributes simultaneously included.

RESULTS

Model I indicates that, among our Leadership Controls, both Journal Leadership and Author Leadership are significant and have negative effects on community performance. Only one of our Prestige Controls, Institution Prestige, is significant and negative, indicating it negatively impacts community performance. Model II introduced the first of our main variables of interest, Community Cohesiveness. We found that cohesive rhetoric was associated with improved performance, while a broad use of knowledge maximized performance. Model III examined the second of our main variables of interest, Community Uniqueness. We found that knowledge communities maximized performance when they used rhetoric similar to that of other clusters, while knowledge (as represented by citations) gathered from diverse sources predicted superior community performance. Model IV used the third of our chief variables of interest, Community Flexibility. We found that, when taken without our prior variables of interest, the flexibility of knowledge communities, in both rhetoric and citations, was not a statistically significant predictor of community performance.

Model V incorporated all the previously discussed variables for a simultaneous examination of their effects on knowledge community performance. We found that all main variables of interest retained the significance and direction found in Models II–III. Additionally, our variables of interest from Model IV became significant predictors and collectively explained 83.5% of the variation in knowledge community performance. The variable for mixed industry/firm affiliation became statistically significant at the $p < .10$ level in this model. Table 2.3 displays a summary of our model coefficients and their statistical significance, and goodness of fit summaries for all five models are presented in Table 2.4.

In all our models, we examined the coefficients of industry affiliation. We found that throughout Models I–V, community performance was enhanced by a high percentage of purely industry-affiliated papers, though in Model III this effect was only significant at the $p < .10$ level. On the other hand, a higher percentage of mixed industry-affiliated papers indicated a slightly negative, and statistically insignificant, impact on community performance. This indicates that the effect of higher proportions of purely academic-affiliated papers is indistinguishable from that of mixed-affiliation papers. Clusters with higher proportions of purely industry-affiliated papers were associated with higher performance than clusters with elevated proportions of either purely academic or mixed-affiliation clusters.

Since our hypotheses examined the use of citations and rhetoric for the same three measures, we then examined the correlation between rhetoric and citation structures for each pair of similar variables. There was a significant, positive relationship between citation and rhetoric measures for all three knowledge community measures. For knowledge community cohesiveness, regressing the similar measures for rhetoric on citations yielded an r^2 of 0.846, indicating that approximately 85% of the variation in rhetorical cohesiveness was attributable to changes in citation cohesiveness. Similarly, for knowledge community uniqueness, the r^2 of 0.4008, approximately 40% of the variation in rhetorical uniqueness, was explained by changes in citation uniqueness. Lastly, an r^2 of 0.9004 for knowledge community flexibility indicated that about 90% of the changes in rhetorical flexibility were explained by corresponding changes in citation flexibility.

Table 2.3   Descriptive statistics

		1	2	3	4	5	6	7	8	9	10	11	12	13	14	15
1	Number of Papers	–														
2	Knowledge Cohesiveness	(0.16)	–													
3	Rhetorical Cohesiveness	0.09	0.92*	–												
4	Knowledge Uniqueness	0.39*	0.26*	0.41*	–											
5	Rhetorical Uniqueness	0.66*	0.23*	0.45*	0.63*	–										
6	Know. Comm. Adaptability Rate	0.71*	0.05	0.27*	0.40*	0.75*	–									
7	Rhet. Comm. Adaptability Rate	0.72*	0.01	0.28*	0.46*	0.80*	0.95*	–								
8	Journal Leadership	0.01	0.17	0.21	0.07	0.24*	0.25*	0.28*	–							
9	School Leadership	0.14	0.81*	0.88*	0.53*	0.57*	0.33*	0.35*	0.19	–						
10	Member Leadership	0.05	0.68*	0.71*	0.47*	0.53*	0.25*	0.28*	0.28*	0.80*	–					
11	Journal Prestige	0.01	(0.17)	(0.18)	(0.35)*	(0.03)	0.04	0.02	0.14	(0.27)*	(0.13)	–				
12	School Prestige	(0.55)*	(0.05)	(0.22)*	(0.57)*	(0.54)*	(0.52)*	(0.55)*	0.05	(0.41)*	(0.25)*	0.46*	–			
13	Member Prestige	(0.46)*	(0.06)	(0.23)*	(0.59)*	(0.54)*	(0.48)*	(0.50)*	0.05	(0.37)*	(0.19)	0.48*	0.82*	–		
14	Pure Industry Affiliation	0.42*	0.32*	0.46*	0.47*	0.74*	0.54*	0.60*	0.42*	0.49*	0.65*	0.05	(0.27)*	(0.26)*	–	
15	Mixed Affiliation	0.42*	0.19	0.36*	0.39*	0.67*	0.59*	0.64*	0.37*	0.42*	0.44*	(0.01)	(0.37)*	(0.38)*	0.64*	–
	Mean	0.60	0.14	0.19	0.02	0.37	0.62	0.81	0.02	0.36	33.91	6.07	8.57	8.65	0.19	0.08
	Std. Dev.	0.44	0.06	0.04	0.01	0.07	0.18	0.17	0.02	0.08	9.18	4.09	5.12	5.17	0.05	0.03
	Min	0.02	0.06	0.14	0.00	0.18	0.10	0.20	0.00	0.18	20.63	1.00	1.00	1.00	–	–
	Max	2.10	0.38	0.33	0.05	0.54	0.93	0.97	0.19	0.63	62	16	21	21	0.35	0.21

Notes: Descriptive Statistics (n = 231, i = 22 clusters, t = 12 years: 1992–2003) Correlations. * Denotes significance at the α = .05 level using the Bonferroni correction for multiple pairwise tests. Number of papers divided by 1,000 to adjust scale. n for adaptability variables is 220.

Table 2.4   Time series GLS estimation

	(I)	(II)	(III)	(IV)	(V)
Cohesiveness					
Knowledge		(1.090) **			(1.032) **
Rhetoric		1.155 *			1.169 **
Uniqueness					
Knowledge			(4.354) *		(4.040) *
Rhetoric			1.536 ***		1.494 ***
Adaptability					
Knowledge				0.173	0.293 *
Rhetoric				(0.004)	(0.272) *
Control Variables					
Lagged Response					
One Year	0.669 ***	0.632 ***	0.591 ***	0.623 ***	0.557 ***
Leadership Controls					
Journal Leadership	(4.715) *	(4.649) *	(3,323)	(4.809) *	(3.240)
School Leadership	0.316 +	0.152	(0.249)	0.213	(0.394)
Member Leadership	(0.006) **	(0.004) +	(0.005) *	(0.005) *	(0.004) *
Prestige Controls					
Journal Prestige	0.006	0.006	(0.001)	0.005	(0.002)
School Prestige	(0.018) **	(0.018) **	(0.018) ***	(0.017) **	(0.019) ***
Member Prestige	0.004	0.004	0.010 *	0.005	0.011 **
Industry/Academy Affiliation Controls					
Pure Industry affiliation	1.528 ***	1.454 ***	0.519 +	1.428 ***	0.599 *
Mixed Industry/Academy Affiliation	(0.340)	(0.518)	(0.823)	(0.508)	(0.858) +
Constant	0.176 **	0.164 **	0.103	0.149 *	0.108
N	231.000	231.000	231.000	231.000	231.000
r-squared	0.794	0.800	0.828	0.798	0.835
Chi-2	1,536.359	1,689.914	2,110.959	1,682.826	2,213.746

Notes: Dependent variable: number of papers published by a community in a given year. *** p <0.001; ** p <0.01; * p <0.05; + p <0.10. Standard errors in parentheses. Number of papers divided by 1,000 to adjust scale.

It is important to note that the trends identified by these measures were consistent throughout the dataset; the extremely high correlations are chiefly due to extreme values. When examining the same regression for knowledge community cohesiveness as above, but including only the central 80% of points, we found that a more reasonable 50% of the total variation in rhetorical cohesiveness was attributable to changes in citation cohesiveness. To ensure that these results retained their significance when controlling for the other previously identified covariates in our full model, we refitted this model, including all variables from our full model, and saw that our relationships remained large, positive, and statistically significant. These findings augment the visual trends in the MDS plots in Appendix 2.2, where it is clear that rhetoric and citations have similar cluster structures and tend to move in tandem.

The large correlations for community cohesiveness and community flexibility indicated that the inclusion of both knowledge and rhetoric variables might cause problems in our regressions as a result of the "wrong sign" problem (Gugarati, 1995). To address these concerns, we examined our models without the paired variables that create these issues.[1]

The strong correlations between rhetoric and knowledge suggest that the use of interaction effects could untangle the nature of the relationships between variables. Specifically, we wondered what the relationship was between the pairs of variables for cohesiveness, uniqueness, and flexibility for knowledge and rhetoric, and also about the relationships between each of these variables and cluster size. We revisited our models, including the interaction effects between pairs of knowledge community variables. For uniqueness, we found that interaction effects were not significant and thus had no impact on our results. For cohesiveness, on the other hand, we found that the interaction effect was more significant than either rhetorical or knowledge cohesiveness variables, and the rhetorical cohesiveness effect no longer supported our question as meaningful. Since both of our variables for cohesiveness were expressed as decimals, it is not surprising that the product of these two variables demanded a larger coefficient to compensate. When the interaction effect for flexibility was added, rhetorical flexibility continued to support our original hypotheses, but citation flexibility fell slightly short of statistical significance. These findings confirm that knowledge and rhetoric have some differential relationship, while four of our six hypotheses remain fully supported.

We also examined the interaction of prior-year cluster size with our knowledge and rhetoric variables. These interactions were largely insignificant, with the only notable exception being the interaction between rhetorical uniqueness and prior-year cluster size. This interaction suggests that the effect of rhetorical uniqueness may be related to the size of the cluster. This could be related to an intrinsic property of clusters or an artifact of variable construction.

These correlations do not negate our findings, but do require us to keep in mind that, when interpreting our regression coefficients, our assumption is that all other variables in the model are held constant. That the use of language and the use of citations are related to each other is not surprising, since authors are citing papers they learned from. Language and source of language are inseparable, as are technical terms, norms of language, socially constructed uses of vocabulary, and so on. On the other hand, language and source of language are not identical—a paper, while it relies on citations, is not a function of them. In order to isolate the effects of language and knowledge sources, we chose to leave out interaction effects in the main models while we remained aware of the care needed in interpreting our results. We believe further research would be very helpful in further exploring these relationships.

ROBUSTNESS

Many additional factors in our analysis have not yet been considered, and our preceding models have a number of limitations. Table 2.5 summarizes the results for the first three robustness checks, and Table 2.6 summarizes the fourth.

First, our original dependent variable was a count of papers published by a cluster in a given year. To focus on the impact of a cluster, we replaced this with the aggregate number of citations received by publications from each cluster in a given year, another powerful measure of the community's success—though we believe this latter quantity emphasizes long-term impact over current performance. As seen in Model II in Table 2.5, the use of Total Citations did not affect the direction of our coefficients; however, only knowledge cohesiveness and rhetorical uniqueness retained their significance.

Second, the use of Total Citations as our dependent variable affords us the unusual ability to subdivide the dependent variable into internal and external measures of impact. We divided the citations received by a cluster into two distinct variables, representing citations received from other papers within the community and citations received from outside the community, and examined these two quantities individually. The results of these analyses are reported in Models III and IV in Table 2.5. While several variables lost significance, in general the directionality of the coefficients confirmed our primary findings. Interestingly, the endo-cites analysis (cites made to other papers in the cluster) seemed to parallel our findings more strongly. These two observations, coupled with our prior checks regarding collinearity, may imply that a knowledge community's success is self-driven. If cluster success is indeed endogenous, the high r^2 values of our internal measures, Community Cohesiveness and Community Flexibility, would be unremarkable because we would expect internal measurements to change together as the community evolves. Perhaps some additional mechanisms influence endo-cite patterns. For example, we notice an unexpected increase in the prestige variables in this analysis, implying that, after controlling for other factors, cluster prestige is deleterious for attracting external citations. We are also struck by the loss of significance of the time-lag variable in the endo-cites analysis. We speculate that perhaps same-cluster authors may have pre-publication access to articles within their field as a result of informal exchanges of working papers, conference presentations, and generally quick diffusion of ideas through their scholarly networks.

Third, we further examined the author leadership measure used in the main analysis. While an eigenvector measure of network centrality, which we used in our main analysis, is a good measure of direct and indirect influence, it uses non-directional ties. We therefore also measured for degree centrality, which included only direct influence and in-degree centrality measures that represented unidirectional influence. These results are displayed in Models V and VI of Table 2.5. We found that the coefficients for all but one of our variables of interest were perfectly consistent, both in direction and significance, with our main model. Knowledge Cohesiveness was not statistically significant in these models. The only other noteworthy change was that in-degree centrality, similar to eigenvector centrality, achieved statistical significance, while degree centrality was not itself statistically significant.

Fourth, we realized that numerous techniques could be validly utilized in modeling our particular form of time-series data. Furthermore, parametric assumptions relating to the variance-covariance structure were specific to each model estimation technique. In order to test the robustness of our results to our choice of models, we fit three statistically viable alternative models: the Random Effects model MLE version, a panel-data GLS model, and a GEE approach. Through these alternative models, we could contrast the coefficients against our chosen model to gauge how our assumptions regarding the correlation and variance-covariance structure of our data influenced our results.

The models differed chiefly in their error and variance-covariance structures. The Random Effects model, estimated in both standard and MLE manners, makes general assumptions common to all least squares methods. This broader assumption is less specific than the

Table 2.5   Robustness table

	(I) Base	(II) Totcites	(III) Endo-cites	(IV) Exo-cites	(V) Degree	(VI) In-degree
Cohesiveness						
Knowledge	(1.032) **	(11.343) **	(6.745) ***	(4.599) *	(1.842) ***	(2.186) ***
Rhetoric	1.169 **	8.188	5.045 *	3.143	1.167 **	1.586 ***
Uniqueness						
Knowledge	(4.040) *	(44.069) $^+$	(24.015) **	(20.054)	(3.308) $^+$	(2.999)
Rhetoric	1.494 ***	13.931 ***	5.713 ***	8.218 ***	1.515 ***	1.297 ***
Flexibility						
Knowledge	0.293 *	1.877	1.071 *	0.806	0.377 **	0.294 *
Rhetoric	(0.272) *	(1.360)	(0.838) *	(0.522)	(0.339) **	(0.283) *
Centrality						
Member Leadership (Degree)					0.008	
Member Leadership (In-Degree)						0.015 *
Control Variables						
Lagged Response						
One Year	0.557 ***	1.566 **	0.403	1.163 $^+$	0.550 ***	0.570 ***
Leadership Controls						
Journal Leadership	(3.240)	(35.194)	(15.535)	(19.658)	(3.140)	(3.338)
School Leadership	(0.394)	(1,215)	0.053	(1.269)	(0.590) *	(0.447) $^+$
Member Leadership (Eigenvector)	(0.004) *	(0.040) *	(0.017) *	(0.023) *		
Prestige Controls						
Journal Prestige	(0.002)	(0.058)	(0.032)	(0.026)	(0.002)	(0.002)
School Prestige	(0.019) ***	(0.152) **	(0.060) *	(0.092) *	(0.018) ***	(0.016) ***
Member Prestige	0.011 **	0.014	0.043 *	(0.029)	0.011 *	0.011 **
Industry/Academy Affiliation Controls						
Pure Industry affiliation	0.599 *	5.997 *	2.335 *	3.662	0.391	0.316
Mixed Industry/Academy Affiliation	(0.858) *	(10.761) *	(3.275)	(7.485) *	(0.917) $^+$	(0.981) *
Constant	0.108	2.651 ***	0.524	2.127 ***	0.104	0.070
N	231	231	231	231	231	231
Chi-2	2,213,746	765.696	508.747	819.769	2,191.543	2,274.363
r-squared	0.835	0.634	0.528	0.641	0.834	0.837

Notes: *** $p < 0.001$; ** $p < 0.01$; * $p < 0.05$; $^+$ $p < 0.10$. Standard errors in parentheses. Number of papers divided by 1,000 to adjust scale s.

panel-data GLS model, which does not force conformity upon correlations and error terms where there could be a more complex structure. The GEE approach avoids considering the variance-covariance structure as a necessity (though it remained an option) in the correct specification of the distribution mean (Diggle et al., 2002; Long, 1997). In fitting our GEE model, we utilized the option of specifying the within-group correlation structure as AR(1) based on our prior results of the Wooldridge test for first-order autocorrelation in panel data. A further positive attribute of both the GEE and the standard Random Effects approaches is the ability to report significance using the robust modified standard errors.

In terms of our earlier model specification, the panel-data GLS model takes on an identical formulation to our GLS random effects model in all regards except for the second term of the errors, denoted T_{zi} in the prior formulation above. This second term is no longer ignored and features the auto-regressive terms based on panel-specific autocorrelations, as shown in the following formula:

$$
T_{zi} = \begin{bmatrix} \sigma_1^2 & \rho_1\sigma_1^2 & \cdots & \rho_1^{n-1}\sigma_1^2 \\ \rho_2\sigma_2^2 & \sigma_2^2 & \cdots & \rho_2^{n-2}\sigma_2^2 \\ \cdots & \cdots & \cdots & \cdots \\ \rho_n^{n-1}\sigma_n^2 & \rho_n^{n-2}\sigma_n^2 & \cdots & \sigma_n^2 \end{bmatrix}
$$

The GEE model is also identical in terms of the specification for the mean; however, the T_{zi} listed above for the panel-data GLS model would remain in the same general form, but with two slight modifications. First, the auto-regressive coefficients are constrained to be identical across all panels (rows) such that $\rho_1, \rho_2, \ldots, \rho_n = \rho$. Second, the values of the σ_{i2} terms are adjusted for group membership, our cluster assignments, according to the Huber-White robust standard error calculations. For a full comparison of these alternative model specifications via the results they generated, see Table 2.6.

Our alternative model specifications yielded remarkably strong support for the robustness of our findings. Across all alternative specifications, the direction and statistical significance of our variables of interest were nearly unchanged. Only knowledge uniqueness lost significance when we utilized a different modeling technique. Interestingly, in both our GLS and GEE models, the measure of pure industry affiliation lost statistical significance, while the measure of mixed industry/academic affiliation became negative and significant.

Our robustness analyses, taken together, provide additional support for our variable choices and add nuance to our previous analyses. In our model comparisons, the consistency of the significance and direction for the coefficients gave us greater confidence that our results were not artifacts of variable construction or model specification. In the next chapter, we discuss the significance and contributions of our statistical findings.

DISCUSSION AND CONCLUSIONS

Our previous empirical results, although they strongly supported all but one of our hypotheses in the affirmative across different model specifications, should be interpreted with some qualifications. The analysis of citations and aggregated paper counts had some limitations. First, for the very recent years and the early 1990s, data are less complete because of less availability of digitalized papers and citations at that time. Second, we observed only those papers in computer science that were in cooperating journals or posted on the Web. But, among computer scientists, access to and knowledge of computers are presumably almost universal.

Table 2.6   Evaluation of model specifications

	(1) RE (Main Model)	(2) MLE	(3) GLS-panel data	(4) GEE
Cohesiveness				
Knowledge	(1.032) **	(1.032) *	(1.053) ***	(1.271) **
Rhetoric	1.169 **	1.169 *	0.969 **	1.588 **
Uniqueness				
Knowledge	(4.040) *	(4.040) *	(0.847)	(1.410)
Rhetoric	1.494 ***	1.494 ***	1.196 ***	1.279 ***
Flexibility				
Knowledge	0.293 *	0.293 *	0.281 ***	0.337 *
Rhetoric	(0.272) *	(0.272) *	(0.249) **	(0.233) *
Control Variables				
Lagged Response				
One Year	0.557 ***	0.557 ***	0.478 ***	0.409 ***
Leadership Controls				
Journal Leadership	(3.240)	(3.240) ***	(1.591) **	(1.522)
School Leadership	(0.394)	(0.394) +	(0.322) +	(0.400)
Member Leadership (Eigenvector)	(0.004) *	(0.004) *	(0.003) +	(0.005) *
Prestige Controls				
Journal Prestige	(0.002)	(0.002)	(0.000)	0.001
School Prestige	(0.019) ***	(0.019) ***	(0.014) ***	(0.017) ***
Member Prestige	0.011 **	0.011 **	0.005	(0.001)
Industry/Academy Affiliation Controls				
Pure Industry affiliation	0.599 *	0.599 *	0.331 +	0.257
Mixed Industry/Academy Affiliation	(0.858) +	(0.858)	(0.865) **	(0.806) **
Constant	0.108	0.108	0.155 **	0.233 *
N	231	231	231	231
Chi-2	2,213.746	416.196	950.264	1,110.231
LL	n/a	61.448	126.399	n/a
r-squared	0.835	n/a	n/a	n/a

Notes: *** $p < 0.001$; ** $p < 0.01$; * $p < 0.05$; + $p < 0.10$. Standard errors in parentheses. Number of papers divided by 1,000 to adjust scale.

The use of citations is also limited as a result of ambiguous interpretations. We take citations to a paper to be a sign that the knowledge in the paper is being built on and added to. However, some studies suggest alternative motives for citation, including social, historical, and representative (Small, 1978). Therefore, the pattern of citations may not perfectly model the intellectual structure of a paper, but it may reflect similarity between individuals if they cite the same seminal works, the same mentors, and so on. We believe that, in aggregate, citations can be seen as a good proxy for influence, but certainly not a perfect one. To check robustness of our citations-based clustering, we did check for the "purity" or amount of in-cluster vs. between-cluster similarity of journals and rhetoric, which should in many cases be highly correlated to content. Our clusters did seem to capture journals and rhetoric well, lending additional support that our clusters are meaningful.

Increased number of papers published in a community may be a sign of community growth, but it is not necessarily a sign of increased community innovation. Our alternative model specifications and our alternative use of total citations as a dependent variable go some way toward mitigating this concern. Some studies have been able to map success to artistic or creative effort, such as Uzzi, Spiro, and Delis's (2005) use of critics and box office success and Fleming et al.'s (2005) contrasts between the conditions that maximize creativity and impact.

Our controls for journal, member, and school prestige were not often positive and significant. Perhaps this points to an even more interesting suggestion that "superstar" scientists may be more prevalent in contexts of emerging or poorly structured knowledge communities. We speculate that the shape of the knowledge community will be significant in determining the structure of credit allocated for innovation as well as the rate of innovation.

We found that knowledge communities with more papers with pure industry affiliations were, overall, more successful and that knowledge communities with more mixed industry/academic affiliations were overall less successful. But the direction of causality here was unclear. The findings indirectly support the findings of Gittelman and Kogut (2003)—who argue that papers with high academic impact tended to be less commercializable because they use competing logics—because having a high proportion of papers in a knowledge community that tries to combine both logics results in less overall success. Similarly, March (1991) argued for the competing logics of exploration and exploitation in research, and it can be imagined that firms would tend to be more interested in the latter (Gittelman & Kogut, 2003; Jayaraj & Gittelman, 2018a, 2018b).

The role that firms play in knowledge communities, particularly as findings from academia become increasingly commercialized, is an interesting and important question (Henderson et al., 1998; Shane, 2002). Industry involvement in a knowledge community might help overall innovativeness, leading to more resources, more support, and new sources of ideas, particularly in an applied field, such as computer science. Or overly strong industry involvement could focus research on short-term usefulness, result in less free communication because knowledge is treated proprietarily, and reduce long-term rates of innovation.

Some radically different modeling techniques could have better illuminated some other aspects of knowledge communities. Future work might test a stochastic modeling approach that uses the history of each particular school of thought to predict its next performance outcome. By ignoring the source of these variations, one could simply focus on how the current status of a school of thought, combined with its past performance, predicts future performance.

Another approach could have independently predicted the birth and death of clusters based on additional factors either from within our model or completely externally generated. A separate process could then free-up our model to focus on the relationships of schools of thought based upon their "life-cycle," considering time relative to the birth of a cluster rather than absolutely. This decomposition of time into independent components could further our understanding of how knowledge communities initially grow, mature, and disappear.

This research, though it focuses on the academic field of computer science, has broad implications for firms. About 30% of the papers in our data were authored by a researcher whose primary identification was a firm. Studies increasingly show spillover between academia and technology (Henderson et al., 1998).

Future research can more clearly delineate the important relationship between firms and knowledge communities, not just firms and scientific research. We predict that firms with researchers participating specifically in successful and innovative knowledge communities will be more likely to generate successful innovation, as valuable knowledge is transferred back into the firm. Similarly, we believe that the ability to identify and predict community success will be a valuable tool for governments trying to encourage promising nascent technology, or even in guiding the rule-setting bodies of government to help encourage productive collaborative networks. Venture capitalists may be interested in identifying what areas of technology are most likely to be productive in order to more efficiently allocate investments. Lastly, given the intertwined success and failure of knowledge communities, researchers may be able to make more intelligent and productive choices when embedding themselves in a research community.

To provide an intuitive example of how this analysis might be understood in a given environment, we identified two clusters with similar recent growth histories, one of which is on the verge of growth while the other is on the verge of shrinkage. If our analysis is correct, the underlying characteristics, in terms of community cohesiveness, uniqueness, and flexibility, may help to predict these outcomes. While this analysis is decidedly ad hoc, it is meant as an illustration rather than a proof of our methodology. In this case, we identified cluster 4, which focuses on the design of cryptographic systems, and cluster 13, which focuses on machine learning (see Appendix Table 2A.1). In 1996, both clusters have similar numbers of papers and have remained stable from the prior years. Underlying this apparent similarity, we observe that cluster 13 has sharply increased in its rhetorical cohesiveness and stability while becoming less rhetorically unique. Cluster 13 has also become more diverse in its use of knowledge while remaining stable in knowledge uniqueness and flexibility. Cluster 4, on the other hand, has become much more rhetorically diverse, grown more focused in its knowledge cohesiveness, and decreased in knowledge flexibility. Overall, our analysis predicts that cluster 13 is primed for growth, while cluster 4 is not. The performance of these clusters over the next three years bears this out, as cluster 13 grows approximately 79% from 1996 to 1999, while cluster 4 shrinks by about 12%. While this is a relatively extreme case, and our findings in this chapter speak of average tendencies that are not necessarily applicable to every case, this example illustrates how our methods might be used practically to understand a cluster's performance.

We have offered a macro-level framework for organizing large-scale innovation networks—called knowledge communities—and attempt to show how persistent community-level characteristics explain their differential success. Knowledge communities are a valuable level of analysis for studying innovation in science and technology.

Not all scientists are part of such "clusters" of cohesive research. Only about 40% of the work in computer science emerges from clusters of scientists who collaborate in producing knowledge. Knowledge communities produce, however, a disproportionate amount of the knowledge in computer science. In our dataset of computer science publications in technical journals, 56.61% of citations are received by papers in clusters, even though only 43.67% of papers are in clusters. This trend is more dramatic within clusters, where 76.16% of citations go from one paper in a cluster to another paper in a cluster. On the other hand, papers not in a cluster cite almost proportionately to the ratio of papers in and out of cluster, with 41.32% of citations going to the 43.67% papers in a cluster and 58.68% of citations going to the 56.33% papers not in a cluster.

Literature on small worlds (Watts, 1999) and geographic clustering (Delgado & Porter, 2021; Porter, 1998; Porter et al., 2004) has begun to address how large-scale networks contribute to productivity. We focus on the way knowledge communities use knowledge and rhetoric to help explain why some of these knowledge communities flourish and grow (Pfeffer, 1993). Building on theory from exploratory search and marketing, we find that the patterns for knowledge use and use of rhetoric are very different. A broad-searching, far-ranging, and flexible use of knowledge maximizes community performance, while a shared, common, and stable rhetoric is most beneficial to community performance. We did not find support for the proposition that the use of unique knowledge benefits knowledge communities. Increased work by authors associated with firms had an overall positive effect on knowledge community performance, but an increase in work done jointly by researchers from firms and academic institutions led to an overall negative effect on knowledge community performance. This is a very good start to establishing that knowledge communities are a coherent and meaningful way to look at innovation over long periods of time. And if we can understand how knowledge communities function and thrive, then this research and these insights could also be potentially important and useful.

NOTE

1. To check Model II for this effect, we kept the same controls and ran the model with both knowledge and rhetorical cohesiveness alone. Each variable retained its direction but became slightly less significant. In Model III, the individual inclusion of each variable saw knowledge uniqueness flip to the positive when included individually; however, it was not statistically significant. This could indicate that our joint significance reveals a secondary trend in knowledge uniqueness that is only evident after controlling for the rhetorical uniqueness of a cluster. Rhetorical uniqueness retains its significance and direction when it is included alone in Model III. In our investigation of Model IV, we found that Knowledge Flexibility retained its significance and direction when included individually, while Rhetorical Flexibility did flip to the positive direction, but without statistical significance. This individual flip explains why the original Model IV, including both variables finds neither to be significant. Finally, to verify that our results in the final model are not unduly influenced by these, we included just one of each pair and found our directions remained fairly consistent with the expected changes in significance already detailed in the earlier models.

APPENDIX 2.1

Table 2A.1   Cluster descriptions and cluster growth by year from 1993 to 2003 for clusters 1–22 (as % of in-cluster papers)

Cluster #	Proposed name for cluster topic	CAGR, 1992–2003	Cumulative # of papers, 1990–2003	Cluster growth by year 1992–2003 as % of in-cluster (x-axis) Change in # of papers between 0% and 15% change per year for clusters 1–21 and 0–100% change for no cluster (y-axis)
5 Most common words (frequency)	*Titles of 3 most cited papers*			
1 – Cluster One	*Machine Learning and Neural Networks*	*-6.83%*	7892	*Machine Learning/Neural Networks*
Learn (1390) Network (691) Robot (649) Neural (606) Model (506)	Finding Structure in Time An Information-Maximization Approach to Blind Separation and Blind Deconvolution Learning to Predict by the Methods of Temporal Differences			
2 – Cluster Two	*Object Oriented Languages*	*-5.06%*	9368	*Object Oriented Languages*
Type (835) Object (821) Program (800) System (709) Language (624)	Aspect-Oriented Programming A Hierarchical Internet Object Cache Logical Foundations of Object-Oriented and Frame-Based Languages			

Cluster #	Proposed name for cluster topic	CAGR, 1992–2003	Cumulative # of papers, 1990–2003	Cluster growth by year 1992–2003 as % of in-cluster (x-axis) Change in # of papers between 0% and 15% change per year for clusters 1–21 and 0–100% change for no cluster (y-axis)
5 Most common words (frequency)				Titles of 3 most cited papers
3 – Cluster Three	*Model Verification*	*–4.16%*	*7022*	*Model Verification*
System (1267) Time (826) Model (783) Verification (435) Specification (434)			Symbolic Model Checking for Real-time Systems; The Algorithmic Analysis of Hybrid Systems; STATEMATE: A Working Environment for the Development of Complex Reactive Systems	
4 – Cluster Four	*Design of Crypto-graphic Systems*	*n/a*	*4144*	*Design of Cryptographic Systems*
System (557) Distribute (524) Protocol (279) Base (222) Fault (220)			A Method for Obtaining Digital Signatures and Public-Key Cryptosystems; A Reliable Multicast Framework for Light-weight Sessions and Application Level Framing; Random Oracles are Practical: A Paradigm for Designing Efficient Protocols	

Cluster #	Proposed name for cluster topic	CAGR, 1992–2003	Cumulative # of papers, 1990–2003	Cluster growth by year 1992–2003 as % of in-cluster (x-axis) Change in # of papers between 0% and 15% change per year for clusters 1–21 and 0–100% change for no cluster (y-axis)
5 Most common words (frequency)	Titles of 3 most cited papers			
5 – Cluster Five	Machine Vision/Graphics	n/a	6053	Machine Vision/Graphics
Image (717) Model (506) Base (483) Recognition (350) Motion (327)	Machine Vision/Graphics Complements to Pattern Recognition and Neural Networks Performance of Optical Flow Techniques Progressive Meshes			
6 – Cluster Six	Constraint Satisfaction	6.17%	6070	Constraint Satisfaction
Model (471) Constraint (425) System (398) Base (389) Algorithm (380)	Constraint Satisfaction Symbolic Model Checking: 10 20 States and Beyond Symbolic Boolean Manipulation with Ordered Binary Decision Diagrams A New Method for Solving Hard Satisfiability Problems			

Cluster #	Proposed name for cluster topic	CAGR, 1992–2003	Cumulative # of papers, 1990–2003	Titles of 3 most cited papers	Cluster growth by year 1992–2003 as % of in-cluster (x-axis). Change in # of papers between 0% and 15% change per year for clusters 1–21 and 0–100% change for no cluster (y-axis)
5 Most common words (frequency)					
7 – Cluster Seven	*Real Time Networks*	*–9.85%*	*3968*	*Real Time Networks*	*Real Time Networks*
Time (1146)				Supporting Real-Time Applications in an Integrated Services Packet Network: Architecture and Mechanism	
Real (908)				The BSD Packet Filter: A New Architecture for User-level Packet Capture	
System (731)				Service Disciplines for Guaranteed Performance Service in Packet-Switching Networks	
Schedule (638)					
Network (302)					
8 – Cluster Eight	*Programming Languages*	*4.4%*	*7743*	*Programming Languages*	*Programming Languages*
Logic (756)				Proof-Carrying Code	
Program (700)				Exokernel: An Operating System Architecture for Application-Level Resource Management	
System (595)				A Framework for Defining Logics	
Proof (485)					
Type (445)					

Cluster #	Proposed name for cluster topic	CAGR, 1992–2003	Cumulative # of papers, 1990–2003	Cluster growth by year 1992–2003 as % of in-cluster (x-axis) Change in # of papers between 0% and 15% change per year for clusters 1–21 and 0–100% change for no cluster (y-axis)
5 Most common words (frequency)	*Titles of 3 most cited papers*			
9 – Cluster Nine	*Internet Traffic Management*	*–9.68%*	*9002*	*Internet Traffic Management*
System (1253) Distribute (743) Network (651) Mobil (474) Perform (461)	Congestion Avoidance and Control Chord: A Scalable Peer-to-peer Lookup Service for Internet Applications On the Self-Similar Nature of Ethernet Traffic			
10 – Cluster Ten	*Data Mining*	*1.85%*	*10180*	*Data Mining*
Data (887) Queries (886) System (777) Base (767) Database (762)	Fast Algorithms for Mining Association Rules Mining Association Rules between Sets of Items in Large Databases The Anatomy of a Large-Scale Hypertextual Web Search Engine (by Google founders Sergey Brin and Lawrence Page, 1998)			

Cluster #	Proposed name for cluster topic	CAGR, 1992–2003	Cumulative # of papers, 1990–2003	Cluster growth by year 1992–2003 as % of in-cluster (x-axis) Change in # of papers between 0% and 15% change per year for clusters 1–21 and 0–100% change for no cluster (y-axis)
5 Most common words (frequency)				*Titles of 3 most cited papers*
11 – Cluster Eleven	*Network Routing*	*39.01%*	*5890*	*Network Routing*
Network (1060) Multicast (750) Service (444) Base (407) Protocol (404)				Random Early Detection Gateways for Congestion Avoidance RTP: A Transport Protocol for Real-Time Applications Dynamic Source Routing in Ad Hoc Wireless Networks
12 – Cluster Twelve	*Parallel Computing*	*-13.59%*	*5990*	*Parallel Computing*
Parallel (1212) Perform (553) Distribute (533) Computing (524) System (458)				Myrinet: A Gigabit-per-Second Local-Area Network Implementation and Performance of Munin Parallel Programming in Split-C

Innovation and knowledge communities

Cluster #	Proposed name for cluster topic	CAGR, 1992–2003	Cumulative # of papers, 1990–2003	Cluster growth by year 1992–2003 as % of in-cluster (x-axis) Change in # of papers between 0% and 15% change per year for clusters 1–21 and 0–100% change for no cluster (y-axis)
5 Most common words (frequency)	Titles of 3 most cited papers			
13 – Cluster Thirteen	*Machine Learning*	13.82%	9566	*Machine Learning*
Learn (1226) Model (911) Network (664) Base (597) Data (543)	Bagging Predictors Support-Vector Networks Experiments with a New Boosting Algorithm			
14 – Cluster Fourteen	*Shared Memory/ Parallel Processing*	n/a	3818	*Shared Memory/Parallel Processing*
Parallel (479) Memory (466) Cache (297) Perform (281) Share (255)	Design and Evaluation of a Compiler Algorithm for Prefetching TreadMarks: Shared Memory Computing on Networks of Workstations Lazy Release Consistency for Software Distributed Shared Memory			

Cluster #	Proposed name for cluster topic	CAGR, 1992–2003	Cumulative # of papers, 1990–2003	Cluster growth by year 1992–2003 as % of in-cluster (x-axis) Change in # of papers between 0% and 15% change per year for clusters 1–21 and 0–100% change for no cluster (y-axis)
5 Most common words (frequency)	*Titles of 3 most cited papers*			
15 – Cluster Fifteen	*Optimization*	*n/a*	*950*	*Optimization*
Algorithm (134) Genet (104) Problem (64) Optimization (57) Network (56)	Davenport-Schinzel Sequences and Their Geometric Applications Performance of Dynamic Load Balancing Algorithms for Unstructured Mesh Calculations Learning Long-Term Dependencies with Gradient Descent is Difficult			
16 – Cluster Sixteen	*Congestion Control*	*76.57%*	*2297*	*Congestion Control*
Network (514) Tcp (347) Control (324) Service (273) Congest (194)	A Crash Course on Markov Chains and Stochastic Stability Equation-Based Congestion Control for Unicast Applications GPSR: Greedy Perimeter Stateless Routing for Wireless Networks			

Cluster #	Proposed name for cluster topic	CAGR, 1992–2003	Cumulative # of papers, 1990–2003	Cluster growth by year 1992–2003 as % of in-cluster (x-axis) Change in # of papers between 0% and 15% change per year for clusters 1–21 and 0–100% change for no cluster (y-axis)
5 Most common words (frequency)	*Titles of 3 most cited papers*			
17 – Cluster Seventeen	*Distributed Computing*	*44.07%*	*2743*	*Distributed Computing*
Network (379) Web (352) Traffic (253) Cache (213) Service (196)	Wide-area cooperative storage with CFS Accessing Nearby Copies of Replicated Objects in a Distributed Environment Overcast: Reliable Multicasting with an Overlay Network			
18 – Cluster Eighteen	*Internet Search*	*51.74%*	*2428*	*Internet Search*
Mine (366) Data (342) Web (229) Base (206) Algorithm (187)	The PageRank Citation Ranking: Bringing Order to the Web (by Google founders Larry Page, Sergey Brin, et al., 1998) Discovery of Multiple-Level Association Rules from Large Databases An Incremental Multi-Centroid, Multi-Run Sampling Scheme for k-medoids-based Algorithms			

Cluster #	Proposed name for cluster topic	CAGR, 1992–2003	Cumulative # of papers, 1990–2003	Cluster growth by year 1992–2003 as % of in-cluster (x-axis) — Change in # of papers between 0% and 15% change per year for clusters 1–21 and 0–100% change for no cluster (y-axis)
5 Most common words (frequency)	Titles of 3 most cited papers			
19 – Cluster Nineteen	Rewrite Systems	n/a	472	Rewrite Systems
Rewrite (44) System (43) Program (42) Constraint (36) Logic (31)	Rewrite Systems A Survey of Program Slicing Techniques A Needed Narrowing Strategy			
20 – Cluster Twenty	Cryptography	28.04%	3289	Cryptography
Secure (413) Key (238) Protocol (200) Computing (195) Scheme (184)	Proof Verification and the Hardness of Approximation Problems A Digital Signature Scheme Secure Against Adaptive Chosen-Message Attacks Simulating Physics with Computers (by physicist Richard Feynman)			

Innovation and knowledge communities

Cluster #	Proposed name for cluster topic	CAGR, 1992–2003	Cumulative # of papers, 1990–2003	Cluster growth by year 1992–2003 as % of in-cluster (x-axis) Change in # of papers between 0% and 15% change per year for clusters 1–21 and 0–100% change for no cluster (y-axis)
5 Most common words (frequency)	*Titles of 3 most cited papers*			
21 – Cluster Twenty-One	*Image Analysis/ Tracking*	*11.44%*	*3043*	*Image Analysis/Tracking*
Base (304) Image (298) Model (290) Recognition (245) Track (216)	Fast Anisotropic Gauss Filtering The Use of Active Shape Models for Locating Structures in Medical Images Location Systems for Ubiquitous Computing			
No Cluster				

APPENDIX 2.2

Table 2A.2   MDS representations of cluster knowledge and rhetoric over time

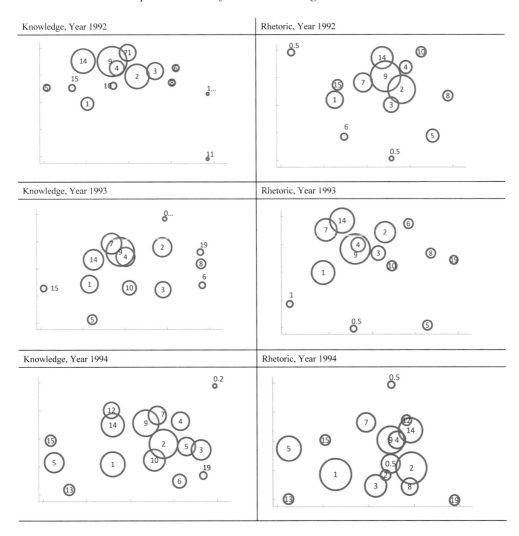

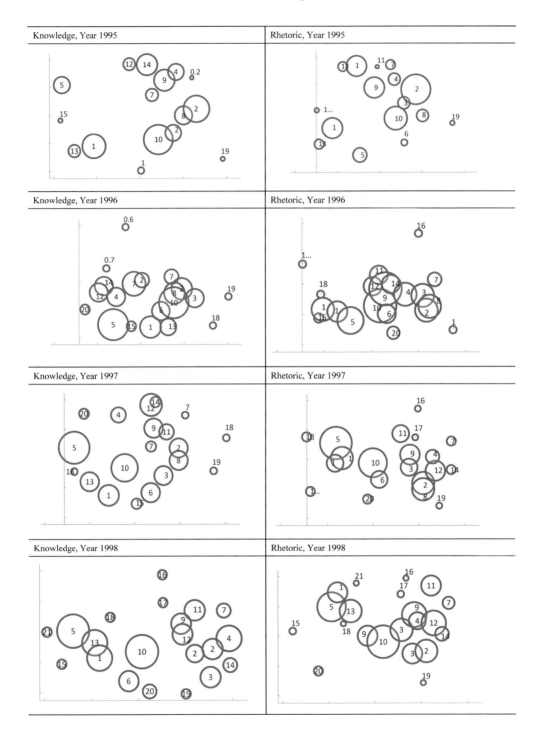

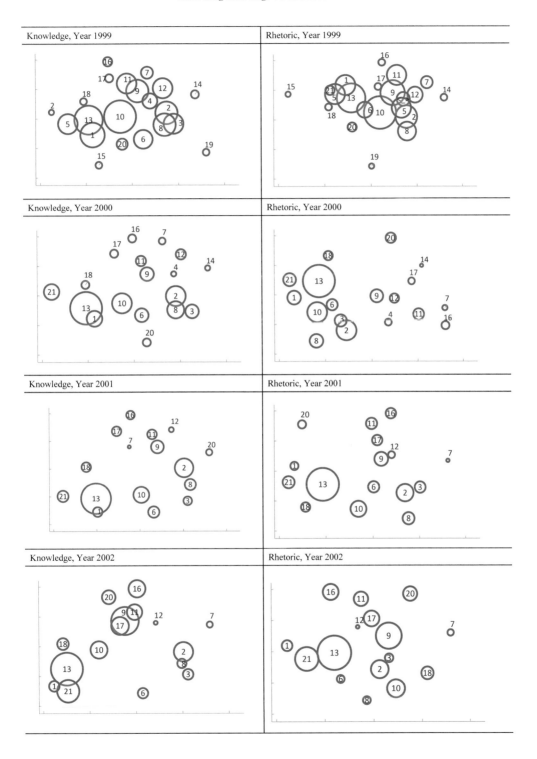

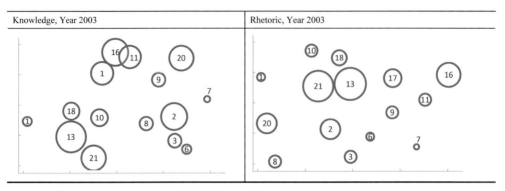

Note: X-Axis and Y-Axis from 0.0-1.0 in 0.2 increments

3. Positioning knowledge: knowledge communities and new knowledge creation

INTRODUCTION AND THEORY

Innovators work in an intellectual and scientific landscape with social structures that shape their actions. In doing so they navigate within, between, and among intellectual knowledge communities that deeply affect their contributions (Kuhn, 1962; Small, 2003, 2018b). Drawing from previous research, we developed a strategic understanding of the positioning incentives for researchers creating new knowledge in the social science field of management, testing whether how scholars interact with their knowledge communities affects their impact. Specifically, we looked at how the position of researchers within or outside knowledge communities relates to the impact of their contributions. We then tested how positioning within knowledge communities and a researcher's experience in multiple knowledge communities affects performance.

As before, we focused on the epistemic community or mini-paradigm of a knowledge community (often called schools of thought in the social sciences)—which we have defined previously as a socially constructed and informal community of researchers who build on each other's ideas, shared similar interests and who, consequentially, share patterns of citation in their work (Crane, 1972, 1980). Research on knowledge communities in citation analysis has been limited but very suggestive (Ennis, 1992; Small & Crane, 1979). While researchers have identified and delineated knowledge communities in various fields, ranging from management of information science to theoretical high-energy physics, they have rarely looked at how these knowledge communities function or how new knowledge performance is affected (Crane, 1980; Culnan, 1987).

The work done within a knowledge community shares intellectual coherency, often accompanied by consistency in methodology, and researchers within a knowledge community tend to read, reference, and influence each other disproportionately. Seminal work by Thomas Kuhn in *The Structure of Scientific Revolutions* argues that groups of researchers with a coherent scientific and intellectual world view and a shared set of questions and methodologies are a fundamental part of intellectual thought and rigor (Kuhn, 1962). In her description of the field of management of information science, Culnan (1986) describes invisible colleges (which we call knowledge communities) as inherent to innovative research: "Researchers in any discipline tend to cluster into informal networks, or 'invisible colleges,' which focus on common problems in common ways. ... The history of the exchanges between members of these subgroups in a discipline describes the intellectual history of the field" (p. 156).

It is perhaps to be expected that loosely defined groups of like-minded researchers within academic fields will tend to study similar questions with overlapping methodologies (Crane,

1989). This holds particularly true in the social sciences, where methodology and goals are fragmented and knowledge communities are prevalent.

Pfeffer (1993), discussing the field of organizational theory, argues that researchers need a strong paradigm to direct and organize the advancement of knowledge through agreed upon goals and vocabulary, so that their work can incrementally build on one another's. He argues that too high a level of external intellectual "borrowing" from outside one's paradigm causes a lack of coherence in a field. As he puts it, "consensus is a critical precondition for scientific advancement" (p. 600). At the opposite extreme, these same forces can socially embed new knowledge builders so that they are structurally disinclined to try to communicate or learn valuable ideas from those outside of their circle, which can lead to intellectual isolation and stagnation.

Knowledge communities can powerfully influence the process of individual knowledge creation, in at least three ways. First, the socially agreed boundaries of knowledge communities influence how developers of new knowledge explicitly think about, and position themselves within, their field; thus, there is an explicit strategic dimension to knowledge positioning (Castro & Lima, 2001). Second, knowledge communities are labels for dense social networks that distribute information through personal ties, conferences, conversations, and so on. They deeply influence the knowledge developer's searches, access to and ease of finding information, and, in aggregate, an individual researcher's knowledge stocks and resulting new knowledge contributions (Doreian, 1988; Moody, 2001). Third, knowledge communities represent mental paradigms that unconsciously influence authors' views of the boundaries of their intellectual world (Crane, 1980; Giest, 2021; Pfeffer, 1993; Small, 2003, 2004).

Factors that encourage successful research are of practical as well as scholarly interest to new knowledge developers (Crane, 1989). Studies by management scholars have used citation analysis to evaluate areas such as journal prestige (Extejt & Smith, 1990; Gomezmejia & Balkin, 1992; Podsakoff et al., 2005; Salancik, 1986; Sharplin & Mabry, 1985), faculty scholarship and institutional productivity (Kirkpatrick & Locke, 1992), and faculty pay (Gomezmejia & Balkin, 1992), and to study the field of management as a cross-disciplinary phenomenon (Blackburn, 1990).

Some management scholars have turned to uncovering the structure of the academic field of management itself. Ramos-Rodriguez and Ruiz-Navarro (2004) describe the development of the field of strategy in the *Strategic Management Journal* from 1980 through 2000; Culnan, O'Reilly, and Chatman (1990) look at the structure of the field of organizational behavior through co-citation techniques; and Üsdiken and Pasadeos (1995) examine the structural divide between European and North American scholars of organizational study. With such meta-analysis, these studies both shape and are shaped by the landscape of current management research (Meyer, 1994).

Knowledge communities contain powerful—but largely unexamined—social, intellectual, and normative mechanisms that influence the impact and direction of knowledge creation (March & Sutton, 1997). The literature, particularly studies of academic research, has not simultaneously examined intellectual structure and performance measures to shed light on the new knowledge development of academic scholars. Nor have previous studies often taken time into account and looked at their fields dynamically. Similarly, while a number of studies in management of information science and bibliometrics delineate fields of scientific and academic study, almost no attention has been given to analyzing whether, and why, being in such a knowledge community is beneficial to its members, and what the advantages and disadvantages of various positions are within and among knowledge communities. This is therefore the goal of this study.

To analyze strategies for maximizing effectiveness in an ideological landscape, we built on the ideas of positioning theorists (Downs, 1957; Hotelling, 1929; McGann, 2002) and search theorists (Cohen et al., 2000; Levinthal, 1997; March & Simon, 1958). Positioning theorists seek to explain the behavior of agents who try to position themselves to appeal to a maximum number of consumers. Search theorists analyze the consequences of local and distant search strategies on outcomes, such as innovation. Using these approaches, we show how the implicit incentive structures created by knowledge communities affect the impact of new knowledge.

The field of study examined in this chapter, micro and macro management strategy, has been characterized throughout its history by competing knowledge communities offering different, and sometimes mutually exclusive, causal explanations for business phenomena and the drivers of firm behavior (Barney, 1986; Mintzberg, 1994). We used a database of 113,000+ papers from 41 top management journals from 1956 to 2002, which covers a critical period in the life of management studies, to explore what affects the impact of the publications of management scholars.

We had three main objectives. First, we wished to understand the systematic mechanisms by which knowledge communities engage and incentivize individual developers of new knowledge. Second, we wished to use citation data to explore how knowledge communities encourage both local and distant search, integrating the findings of recent innovation literature with our theory. Third, we wanted to quantitatively explore the consequences on intellectual impact of new knowledge positioning, both within and between knowledge communities by examining the intellectual organization of the field of management. We hoped to better understand how knowledge is created, identify factors that help determine its impact, and suggest potential avenues of study for future researchers.

Positioning Theory

Hotelling (1929) described a competitive game that was later adapted to explore strategic positioning in ideological space. In the game, two hypothetical newspaper sellers, competing for readers who are distributed evenly along "Main Street," can set up their stand anywhere in town. Assuming that, for the same price, customers will buy the closest newspaper, if one newspaper seller were to position himself anywhere but the center of Main Street, the other would position himself a little closer to the center point and gain the majority of the customers. Thus, both sellers end up converging at the midpoint of Main Street. In this model, each player explicitly takes into consideration the moves of other players when acting. A political variant of this principle was applied to the ideological landscape of voters to explain the middle-of-the-road views generally espoused by candidates of major political parties (Downs, 1957). Given an even distribution of voters, politicians in a two-party race, in order to appeal to the greatest number of voters, will converge to mainstream positions where they maximize their access to voters in a Nash equilibrium. More generally, Downs' work finds that, in an intellectual landscape, given Hotelling's assumptions, a central position closest to the greatest number of consumers is optimal.

Further extending Hotelling's theory, Downs (1957) also challenged the assumption of a "normal" distribution of consumers. Other researchers have further extended Hotelling's game by including multiple players or additional consumer (voter) or competitor (candidate) entry (Krishna, 2001; McGann, 2002). The Hotelling–Downs framework has been usefully applied broadly to such areas as marketing and brand positioning (Choi, 2004), news coverage (Gasper, 2005), and simulations (Marks & Albers, 2001).

The principles of acting to maximize intellectual proximity to the greatest number of consumers, and of employing a dynamic strategy that takes others' moves into consideration, provide a powerful framework for analyzing new knowledge development. The strategic positioning of new knowledge developers explored in this chapter resembles a very complex multi-player version of the Hotelling problem—one, however, that differs along two key dimensions. First, we attempted to include the dimension of knowledge communities, which makes the landscape "clustered" and has profound consequences for the application of Hotelling's strategic principles. Second, in our framework the candidates and the voters were flip sides of the same coin; each producer of new knowledge is also a consumer of new knowledge in our knowledge landscape, simultaneously competing with and supporting the other. In the context of new knowledge development, the positioning theory model significantly underestimates the importance of knowledge communities in the knowledge landscape.

Search Theory: Near and Distant

The tension between local and distant search has been explored by juxtaposing the strategies of exploration and exploitation (March, 1991). Exploration (involving distant search) is an attempt to add value by finding a new opportunity, while exploitation (involving local search) involves building on existing resources or knowledge in an attempt to extract value. Search strategies have significant effects on the development and structure of their landscape (Levinthal, 1991, 1997, 1998). In the long term, exploration does produce benefits, but it must be "paid for" by exploitation (Barnett & Sorenson, 2002). In the shorter term, and from a research perspective, interdisciplinary research—explorative by its very nature—increases the difficulty of publishing papers, training graduate students, or receiving funding for a subject (Birnbaum, 1981b).

However, since the dichotomy between exploration and exploitation is always operationally dependent on the choice of boundary, the way in which we delineate boundaries will determine whether we define a search as near or distant. A number of studies examine the tradeoffs of different search strategies, but they define their relevant boundaries of analysis in different ways. Katila and Ahuja (2002) argue that firms can differentiate themselves by creatively and meaningfully reusing old technology to create new knowledge as well as by finding new technologies to achieve breakthroughs. Nerkar (2003) sees firms successfully choosing between recent, cutting-edge knowledge and knowledge that integrates understandings developed across time spans. Rosenkopf and Nerkar (2001) use patent data to argue that exploration by an optical disk firm that spans organizational boundaries (i.e., involving technologies unfamiliar to the organization), but not technological boundaries, has the most impact within the optical disk industry. They thus differentiate between middle-level and radical exploration. Overall, these researchers find that search patterns have profound effects on knowledge creation. This previous research is tied together by the core idea that when new knowledge is developed, some boundary—internal or external—is extended or challenged.

Although theories of local search often take for granted that there is local and distant knowledge, what makes knowledge accessible and close or inaccessible and far, is left unexplored from an intellectual, psychological, and resource point of view. Delineating these boundaries is indeed a complex process. We argue that a key part of this intellectual boundary-shaping in knowledge development can be found in socially constructed knowledge communities. Knowledge within a knowledge community is readily available and more likely to be the result of "exploitative" searches, while knowledge from other knowledge communities, particularly unrelated ones, will tend to be the result of more "explorative" searches. We believe that knowledge communities are a key factor for new knowledge developers in perceiving information as near or far, and we believe that an appropriate intermediate spanning of boundaries between knowledge communities is an important potential driver of knowledge creation. By providing an explanation for why new knowledge is close or far, we believe we move toward generalizing and integrating previous research on boundary-spanning in knowledge creation.

HYPOTHESES

To understand how an innovator interacts with a knowledge community, we tried to answer (using data) specific questions on how innovators position themselves within a knowledge community. If we find that how they position themselves within a community has enormous impact on their success (whether or not they are aware of this positioning), then there is reason to believe that these knowledge communities are real and potentially deserve more attention and study. Theorists too often study a phenomenon without asking whether they can integrate the macro (group behavior) and the micro (individual incentives) logic. In the case of knowledge communities, there is no leader or codified rules (bylaws), as there is with a formal organization, as a starting point. Rather, we tried to explore whether the incentive structure of the individuals in the group can explain the group behavior we observed. We found it useful to ask questions about incentives of authors and researchers within knowledge communities, and how they might interact with the larger phenomena we were studying. We began with theory and posited questions; we then tested these questions in our dataset.

In this chapter, we posed three hypotheses about the relationship between the position of new knowledge within a knowledge community and the subsequent impact of that knowledge. First, we argued that being part of a knowledge community increases intellectual impact (hypothesis 7). Indeed, most new knowledge is not in any knowledge community at all. Second, we argued that a position near the semi-periphery of a knowledge community (but still within the knowledge community) leads to greater overall impact of new knowledge (hypothesis 8). Third, we argued that, over time, an author's tendencies to explore between knowledge communities, that is, whether a knowledge developer tends to explore many different paradigms or specialize within a paradigm, will affect the impact of his or her ideas (hypothesis 9).

As we have discussed, knowledge communities (or schools of thought) are collaborative groups around common research interests and entail the sharing of information and mutual helping behavior (Crane, 1972). Unlike typical communities, which are usually based primarily on geography, institutional affiliation, or professional boundaries, knowledge communities are based on a shared world view.

A knowledge community creates mechanisms of at least three kinds that keep members at arm's length from other knowledge communities, rewarding members and punishing those who are not members. First, a knowledge community can create a "private language" (Kripke, 1982)—phrases or words that are opaque or unfamiliar to those outside the knowledge community, or a set of methodologies common to it. As Lodahl and Gordon (1972) put it, "high consensus … provides an acceptable and shared vocabulary for discussing the content of the field" (p. 61). Often the vocabulary, the methods, and even the ways of framing problems, are specific to a field and difficult for an outsider to replicate without significant investment. Second, a knowledge community can become detached from other areas of the world by structuring the incentives of its domain through emotional, formal, or reputation-based mechanisms to maintain commitment to its world view (Merton, 1972). Third, a knowledge community can create a world view or paradigm that makes other views ideologically incompatible without substantial theoretical revision, thus making it difficult for others to incorporate or combine the knowledge community with other knowledge communities (Crane, 1980).

Researchers studying communities of practice, which share many characteristics with knowledge communities, have examined how information on performing tasks in such communities is shared informally (Brown & Duguid, 2000; Wenger, 1998). Brown and Duguid (1991) argue that "the ways people actually work usually differ fundamentally from the ways organizations describe that work in manuals, training programs, organizational charts, and job descriptions" (p. 40). These communities have the interesting property that only insiders can fully understand what is being carried out, since no document or set of codified rules exists. Membership in a knowledge community comes at a cost: it must be earned through time-consuming practice and hard-won reputation; and it is hard to fake.

Being a member of a knowledge community can confer significant advantages, allowing a new knowledge developer to embed his or her ideas in powerful methods, tap well-developed shared bases, and gain access to resources and support. In a related project, Powell et al. (1996) saw alliances as an "admissions ticket" to an informal network of learning among corporations. More generally, such networks of learning can offer members invaluable access to learning, financial support, and intellectual underpinnings. Further, people are especially attentive to their special interests and will tend to read pieces that pertain strongly to them (Birnbaum, 1981b). Members of a knowledge community have a well-versed and receptive audience, on which they can build and that allows them to "stand on the shoulders" of one another. Additionally, there are social consequences to being part of a knowledge community, such as the opportunity for repeated interaction and familiarity that is necessary for reputation, trust, and a sense of belonging. Outside of a knowledge community, new knowledge has a harder time finding an audience or building on an intellectual tradition (Birnbaum, 1981a; Small, 1999).

The social and intellectual advantages conferred by knowledge communities warp the intellectual landscape, making it less advantageous to be outside a knowledge community, even if such central, between-cluster positions make sense in a Hotelling positioning framework. While the positioning approach maximizes closeness to a large audience, this "closeness" does not account for the invisible social boundaries of knowledge communities that reward those within them. For these reasons, we do not believe such middle-ground positioning at the "center" of a landscape—the equilibrium, according to Hotelling—will be optimal without taking into consideration knowledge communities. We believe that creators of new knowledge have a strong incentive to position themselves as a part of a specific knowledge community in order to maximize their impact (Birnbaum, 1981a; Stigler, Stigler, & Friedland, 1995).

Hypothesis 7. New knowledge has more impact if it is within a knowledge community than if it is not.

Given that new knowledge is part of a knowledge community, within that knowledge community it can also be at the "core" or "periphery." New knowledge that is core to its knowledge community is consistent with the rest of the knowledge community in its sources of ideas; new knowledge that is peripheral, draws on knowledge that differs in some significant way, usually uncommon knowledge or knowledge from outside the knowledge community (Figure 3.1). We believe that while new knowledge creators receive benefits from being in a knowledge community, membership can also be constraining if they blind themselves to good ideas outside that knowledge community. Specifically, we believe successful research usually draws from its own knowledge community and also a few core ideas from one or two other knowledge communities, synthesizing knowledge that is near and distant. In the area of technological innovation, studies have shown that patents that combine technologies from different patent classes tend to have more diverse, and potentially greater, impact (Trajtenberg, 1990).

Research in local and distant searches suggests that new knowledge that is core to its knowledge community is likely to be intellectually embedded within that knowledge community and have less impact outside of that it. New knowledge located closer to the periphery of its knowledge community tends to more explicitly engage ideas meaningful both to its own field and to audiences beyond its field (McCain, 1986a, 1987). Even within a knowledge community, new knowledge that remains too close to the core ideas and does not search for and use new ideas, is less likely to have innovative impact (Fleming, 2001; Fleming & Sorenson, 2001; Meyer & Zucker, 1989). It is thus less likely to influence others and be more highly cited by those within its knowledge community (Rosenkopf & Nerkar, 2001).

At the same time, as argued in hypothesis 7, new knowledge that is not within a knowledge community tends to attract fewer helpful colleagues, has a harder time drawing on methodologies, and does not have a built-in world view, resulting, on average, in less impact on future knowledge. This implies a tension between being within a knowledge community but still drawing from outside that knowledge community to introduce new ideas and make fresh combinations and contributions (Uzzi & Spiro, 2005).

Network and "small world" theorists have emphasized the advantages of networks of association with groups of tightly connected clusters when bridged by boundary spanners (Reagans, Zuckerman, & McEvily, 2004). These tight cluster formations allow for the small size and repeated interactions that help reputations to develop, and thus also serve as a basis of social capital. When new knowledge is both within a knowledge community and has some connections to other clusters and ideas, these advantages coexist and are maintained. In this case, the advantages of closed network structures, including the maintenance of reputation, learning, and trust, coexist with the advantages of interaction across groups, including new ideas, variation, and synthesis (Burt, 1977). Uzzi et al. (2005) define the curvilinear middle ground between excessive inbreeding and excessive newness as a "cradle of creativity." They draw on Watts' (1999) small world approach to examine this dynamic and illustrate the potential value of moderate levels of familiarity for developing norms, establishing causality, and refining core competencies, as well as the value of new sources for radical innovation and fresh ideas.

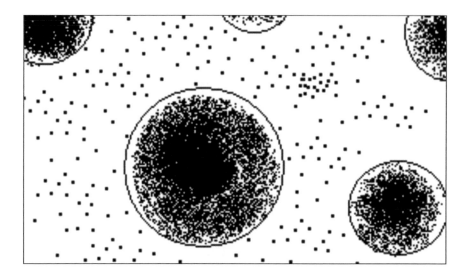

Note: The circles above represent knowledge communities and the dots represent units of knowledge (in this case papers) in relative distance to the centroid of their knowledge communities and other units of knowledge.

Figure 3.1   Knowledge can be positioned within or outside of a knowledge community

Previous findings in search and network theory drive the intuition that knowledge developed with centrality to a knowledge community will tend to have impact largely on that knowledge community only. Conversely, knowledge developed with a peripheral relationship to a knowledge community tends to be accessible and influential to both those in the knowledge community and those beyond it. At the same time, a position that is too far on the periphery risks losing the advantages of being in a knowledge community. This would imply that the relationship between a position at the center and periphery of a knowledge community is curvilinear—that a position at the semi-periphery of a knowledge community, straddling more than one knowledge community or reaching beyond one's knowledge community, would tend to draw the largest audience for new knowledge and receive the most overall citations (Figure 3.2). Such boundary-spanning research is more likely to draw fresh, interesting outside work into a knowledge community, which would potentially result in higher impact.

Hypothesis 8. A position toward the intellectual semi-periphery of a knowledge community results in greater new knowledge impact than a position at the center or periphery of a knowledge community.

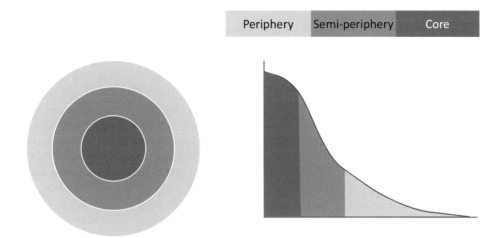

Figure 3.2   Knowledge can be positioned in the periphery, semi-periphery, or core of a knowledge community

We wanted to take into consideration the characteristics of the new knowledge and the exploratory tendencies of creators of new knowledge. Over time, a researcher has a tendency either to explore a diversity of knowledge domains or to focus on one. For example, in the field of economics, Oliver Williamson has published most of his works in one knowledge community—transaction-cost economics (Williamson, 1975, 1979, 2017)—and he is intellectually central to that knowledge community. At the same time, some great new knowledge producers systematically publish works in different fields and are enormously and broadly influential. James March, a peripatetic management scholar who studies organizations, for example, also publishes widely in many knowledge communities, including decision theory, organizational learning, and adaptation (March, 1991; March & Shapira, 1987; March & Simon, 1958).

Ron Burt has argued that "theory developers" focus on deepening and refining theory within one field, while "theory synthesizers" span organizational and knowledge boundaries to combine knowledge in fresh and innovative ways (Burt, 1977). Researchers have examined new knowledge from an author perspective to argue, for example, that authors' geographic location and partner prestige affect impact (Gittelman, 2003), tenure evaluation (Garfield, 1983), and readership (Siggelkow, 2001).

The advantages of remaining within a community are well established in network theory; as discussed above, they include trust, reputation, and learning, among other social and intellectual benefits. Further, learning the norms and knowledge structure of a knowledge community is an investment that may have to be paid again if one changes knowledge community. Simultaneously, from the perspective of influence of an idea, one could argue that remaining in a knowledge community may cause lesser impact after an initial introduction of that idea, whereas a specific idea can be made new many times if transported to different fields (Adner & Levinthal, 2000; Amir, 1985).

In evolutionary economics, the idea of "local search," or search where there is high familiarity, expertise, or current knowledge, is seen as fundamental to developing core competencies and leveraging strengths (Cohen et al., 2000). The implication is that local search reinforces and develops an area of expertise. On the other hand, adopting a strategy that is best according to local searches, but is suboptimal from the perspective of a broader context, can leave an agent stranded on "local peaks" (Cohen et al., 2000; Levinthal & Warglien, 1999; March & Simon, 1958).

New knowledge developed without fresh input and without looking further than itself would be in danger of missing important insights, or as Rosenkopf and Nerkar (2001) put it, might "lead firms to develop 'core rigidities' or fall into 'competence traps'" (p. 288). An innovator may try to avoid falling into such traps by exploring numerous knowledge communities seriously, interacting with a broad array of knowledge in multiple fields. Francis Crick, known for his work on the structure of DNA, seems to believe such theory-hopping is essential for creative insight when he argues that "professional [scientists] know that they have to produce theory after theory before they are likely to hit the jackpot. The very process of abandoning one theory for another gives them a degree of critical detachment that is almost essential if they are to succeed" (Crick, 1988, p. 142).

Serious interaction with multiple knowledge communities may help to expose a new knowledge producer to ideas that can be synthesized, to bridge a structural gap by transporting an idea from an area where it is recognized to one where it is not. Burt (1977) argues that heterogeneity between communities is often greater than within them, and so, where new ideas and diversity are valued, boundary spanners can often learn more by moving between or bridging communities than by remaining within them (Figure 3.3). At the same time, knowledge developers who fail to interact seriously and repeatedly with a knowledge community will not gain the full benefits that such an intellectual and social community can provide, while also sacrificing the learning cost of entry.

We believe that the interests and history of an author, whether eclectic or focused, make a difference to his or her impact and readership. We find that two strong and competing hypotheses are supported in the affirmative by existing theory. On one hand, authors who publish widely and are involved in the intellectual pursuit of multiple areas lend themselves in their eclectic pursuits to the benefits of knowledge combination, and thus gain the advantages of synthesizing between knowledge communities (Fleming, 2001). On the other hand, depth of expertise lends itself to more incremental new knowledge production, gaining the advantages of a closed cluster, so perhaps focusing on one area can be more beneficial to a new knowledge creator (Birnbaum, 1981a, 1981b).

Hypothesis 9a: New knowledge created by those who actively engage in multiple knowledge communities over time has greater impact.

Hypothesis 9b: New knowledge created by those who concentrate on very few knowledge communities over time has greater impact.

Central to our analysis is the idea that new knowledge development is often a result of the constant dynamic tension within the area of a knowledge community between the search for synthesis (i.e., recombination, introducing new ideas) and specialization (i.e., developing the world view of the field, deepening the core methods or proposition of a paradigm). Moreover, scholars face strategic choices in positioning themselves within and among knowledge communities.

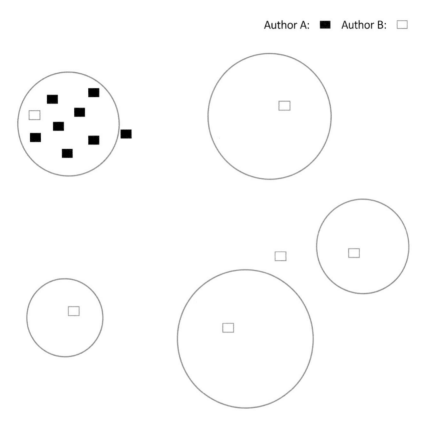

Figure 3.3   *Creators of new knowledge can focus on one knowledge community or jump between knowledge communities*

METHODS, DATA, AND VARIABLES

Clustering Methodology

As discussed previously, co-citation analysis has been used to systematically map and examine the network structures of research papers or patents since Small and Griffith (1974) introduced the first computerized method to accomplish this. A little later, Small and Crane (1979) used large-scale clustering techniques to isolate and identify the structure of scientific disciplines. They thus matched a potent methodology with a coherent intellectual explanation for the "clusters" that Small and Griffith observed during earlier research.

In management research, clustering is usually used to identify similarity between groups of similar firms by technical characteristics, products, or alliance structure. Management scholars have typically used either CONCOR or simple agglomerative techniques to cluster. These methods, developed decades ago, often produced meaningful results, particularly in relatively small, low-dimensional, and cleanly differentiated groups (both methods are supported by UCINET).

Both classes of approaches were designed to be computationally efficient and can be biased by initial clustering choices (by initial merges or splits). CONCOR, which uses matrix convergence to split data into two groups repeatedly, is particularly prone to bias based on initial splits which, once made, are irreversible. For example, Tsai (2002) used CONCOR to study employee coopetition within firms, Hagedoorn and Duysters (2002) to cluster firms based on alliances, and Gerlach (1992) to cluster intercorporate relationships in Japan. Agglomerative clustering is methodologically more intuitive because it compares all agents to each other and merges the most similar ones. It can result in long "chained" clusters if single-link similarities are used and, regardless of parameters, often results in path dependency as a result of initial clustering choices. This method was effectively used in an influential article by Nohria and Garcia-Pont (1991) to differentiate between two firm-organizing principles—firm capabilities and firm alliances. The authors checked their results with another clustering program, kmeans, to confirm that they were meaningful. Both of these methods, as well as other ad hoc single-pass methods that minimize within-cluster distance (Aharonson et al., 2004), are highly prone to clustering path dependency. They work adequately on smaller datasets with clear divisions and limited clustering characteristics (dimensions). But, particularly in large, complex, and high-dimensional data, they are non-transparent and can lead to potentially inaccurate and counterintuitive clusterings.

Increasingly sophisticated methods have been developed in technical and scientific fields to cluster and analyze high-dimensional similarities in enormous databases. These methods take advantage of greater computational power and the potential for multiple passes over the data during clustering (Kandylas, 2005; Kandylas, Ungar, & Forster, 2005; Pantel & Lin, 2002; Popescul et al., 2000). They can fruitfully be applied to management and can result in superior clustering results. To find similar clusters of papers in our data, we drew from advances in Internet search and genetic data mining, to construct a clustering methodology called StrEMer. StrEMer is substantially faster than, and of comparable quality to, past search and mining methods for estimating high-dimensional similarity clusters, and takes into consideration our theoretical model for knowledge communities.

Our criteria were demanding and not met by existing methods. First, we needed a methodology that allowed us to take into account how clusters changed over time, since we wanted to look at data over decades. Second, we needed a methodology that allowed for a substantial portion of our data to not belong to a cluster, since our theoretical framework saw only a portion of new knowledge as belonging to cohesive intellectual clusters. Third, we wanted our framework to include as few arbitrary parameters as possible, letting the data find its own structure. Lastly, without sacrificing accuracy, we wanted our approach to handle extremely large and high-dimensional datasets as efficiently and elegantly as possible.

Most current popular clustering programs in computer science, search, and genetic data mining assume that clusters over time are static (Popescul et al., 2000)—that is, that all clusters exist at the beginning and end of the time period under consideration and that no new ones are formed in the interim. This is a tolerable simplifying assumption for short periods in stable environments but more troubling for data over time in a dynamic environment where we must consider emerging clusters, merging clusters, and dying clusters. To address this, we built an iterated "overlapping" clustering methodology into our algorithm that re-clustered in overlapping 10-year blocks, stepping forward by one year at a time. Therefore, the elements in year 1990 would be clustered based only on the elements in 1980 to 1990; papers in year 1991 would be clustered based only on 1981 to 1991, and so on. Thus, the cluster structure of the data in 1975 could be very different from that of 1995. This allows for new clusters to be created and for existing clusters to merge or wither away, while the overlapping 10-year time span enforces some continuity on the clusters over time. This reclustering strategy helps capture the dynamic and evolving nature of clusters.

Further, unlike less efficient iterated programs, such as kmeans and expected maximization algorithms, our StrEMer approach allowed us to set criteria that gave bounds on the error of single-pass algorithms. In this way, it is similar to the streaming clustering approach (Guha et al., 2003), though it uses less restrictive assumptions (Kandylas, 2005). The Clustering by Committee (CBC) approach allows for background clusters but does not have a clear criterion being optimized and overparameterizes the algorithm for our purposes (Kandylas, 2005; Pantel, 2002).

The StrEMer clustering algorithm maximizes the coherence of the clusters, as specified by an objective function measure. Objects to be clustered are initially assigned to clusters by a random procedure, and maximization is achieved by reassigning each object to the existing cluster with the most similar centroid (which is the sum of the similarity of the objects in a cluster). The whole process is repeated until the objective function cannot be substantially improved, considerably reducing path dependency based on initial clusters. Essentially, our method plotted citation (network) structure in high-dimensional space and used the objective function to minimize the distance from the nearest centroid for all papers simultaneously. Distance represents the angle between the vector representing the paper and the centroid of the cluster it is placed in.

Our StrEMer program accomplished clustering in three steps (repeated when doing iterated "overlapping" clustering). In Step I, we made a single pass over the data and constructed several rough clusters. In Step II, we got a collection of high-quality clusters, called committees, based on the clusters obtained in Step I. These committees were tight and not similar to each other, which meant they had high intergroup similarity and low intra-group similarity. In Step III, we either assigned each element to its most similar clusters, or added it to the residue list if it was not similar enough to any cluster.

(See Appendix 3.1 for a graphical display of the clusters we found in our data over time from 1971 to 2002. See Appendix 3.2 for details and pseudocode of the clustering methodology we developed and implemented to cluster this data)

Data

We examined micro and macro management scholarship—a fast-moving, relatively young, and highly fragmented academic field, taught in business school, which is known for its diversity of ideas and its vigorous knowledge communities (Abrahamson, 1996; Abrahamson & Piazza, 2019; Meyer, 1999; Piazza & Abrahamson, 2020). To select our data, we began with previous rankings of journals in management. Coe and Weinstock (1969) established a list of 15 of the most highly respected management journals and later, through interviews with management department chairpersons (Coe & Weinstock, 1984), added seven journals to the list. Sharplin and Mabry (1985) developed a weighted measure of the top 10 leading management journals by calculating a "citation impact efficiency" metric that measures the "number of citations per 10,000 words published annually in either *Administrative Science Quarterly* or the *Academy of Management Journal*" (p. 139). Podsakoff et al. (2005) used previous lists to construct a list of the journals that had the most current influence, resulting in a list of 28, including some added as top specialty journals. This study found that, between 1981 and 1999, the top seven journals in management received 61% of citations and the top 14 journals received 82% of citations. There is evidence that methods, such as co-citation and clustering, do in fact overlap heavily with experts' intuition about the field's boundaries (Lenk, 1983).

Others since Sharplin and Mabry have refined the methods and lists as the field of strategy has evolved and grown. Johnson and Podsakoff (1994) generated a core list, from these disparate (and highly overlapping) lists, by including any journal that is counted by more than one of these lists, excluding some of the ad hoc specialty journals added by Podsakoff et al. (2005). Following this strategy, we found 41 core journals in management (see Tables 3.1 and 3.2). Accessing the Thomson ISI database, we have collected complete sets of all articles and their citations for these 41 journals since 1956. This list of 41 journals includes the field of management, both the macro (which is heavily influenced by economics and sociology) and the micro (which is heavily influenced by psychology) specialties (see Table 3.1). The journals in the ISI database published since 1956 yielded a total of 113,014 papers for analysis—the most complete database in this area compiled, to our knowledge. The papers included over two million citations in the bibliographies of these articles and more than 1.5 million citations were made to these articles (see Table 3.2).

Table 3.1   Fields in which papers in our study fall (as specified by ISI classification of journal)

Citations Received	Papers	Average Cites/Paper	Field
921,507	40,392	22.81	Psychology
357,996	42,193	8.48	Management
350,254	5,737	61.05	Behavior
181,531	27,063	6.71	Sociology & Anthropology
51,692	9,081	5.69	No Category
38,089	12,176	3.13	Economics
14,284	2,059	6.94	Political Science & Public Administration

Note: All citation counts as of 2002.

Bibliometrics, or the quantitative study of bibliography, uses as its unit of analysis the citations made from a published piece of work to other published pieces of work. This methodology is attractive for its impersonality, objectivity, replicability, and scalability (Culnan, 1986). Bibliometric analysis generally relies on the assumption that citations are a good proxy for influence. Similarly, almost all studies using patents use patent citation as a proxy for patent success (Trajtenberg, 1990). In paper-citation work, it is commonly assumed that a citation in a specific piece of work indicates intellectual influence on the published work and value to the citing author (Small, 1978). This may not always be the case, though, as a well-known citation may be used simply to "represent" a point of view, or citations may be made for social reasons. The rigors of the review process and the well-documented correlation between citations and other measures of influence, however, lead us to believe that citation metrics are at least a useful proxy for influence (Bayer & Folger, 1966; Cole & Cole, 1967; Osareh, 1996). Tables 3.1 and 3.2 summarize our data.

Variables

Our unit of analysis was individual papers. Our variables therefore described characteristics of papers, both descriptions of them and also how they relate to other papers published at that time.

Bibliography Size—To control for the increasing number of citations made in papers, we controlled for the number of entries in a paper's bibliography. As seen in Figure 3.4a, the average bibliography size increased steadily over the time spanned by our data.

Total Citations—For our dependent variable, we measured the total impact of a paper as the number of citations it received subsequent to its publication through 2002 (Figure 3.4b).

Year of Publication—We created dummy variables for each year from 1956 to 2002.

Journal of Publication—Because different journals tend to receive different citation rates as a result of varying size of readership and journal prestige, we included dummy variables for each of the 41 journals in our data (Table 3.2 and Figure 3.5).

Co-authorship (Binary)—We included a binary variable for whether a paper has more than one author (1 if co-authored, 0 if single author). This helped control for the differences in the process of joint and individual knowledge production. Almost 34% of the papers in our data were co-authored.

Cluster (Binary)—This binary variable was coded 1 if the paper was in a cluster of other similar papers (representing a "knowledge community") when it was published, and 0 if the paper was not in a cluster when it was published. A little over half of our papers did not belong to any cluster.

Distance—A paper was central to its cluster when its citation structure was very similar to the mean of the citation structure of all papers in its cluster (the centroid). Papers that were typical of their clusters had small distances. Papers that differed from the rest of the group by citing outside sources or by citing uncommonly cited papers had larger distances. We measured distance as the angle υ of the vector representations between the citation structure of a paper and the centroid of its cluster (See Figure 2.1). Papers not in a cluster were not assigned a distance.

Because clusters were generated with data from the year of the paper and the nine previous years, $t^{(-10)}$ to $t^{(0)}$, distance represents the centrality of the paper to its cluster historically at the time of publication, not the centrality of the paper after publication.[1] We also included a second-order effect for distance to capture curvilinearity.

Table 3.2   Journals and summary statistics

Citations Received	Papers	Average Cites/Paper	Journals
297,182	7,775	38.22	Journal of Personality and Social Psychology
195,697	3,530	55.44	Psychological Bulletin
154,557	2,207	70.03	Psychological Review
131,085	14,509	9.03	American Journal of Psychology
93,836	8,039	11.67	American Sociology Review
91,083	4,636	19.65	Journal of Applied Psychology
64,297	4,470	14.38	Management Science
60,031	10,948	5.48	American Journal of Sociology
55,953	2,991	18.71	Administrative Science Quarterly
49,606	2,360	21.02	Academy of Management Journal
32,756	1,501	21.82	Academy of Management Review
31,554	1,283	24.59	Strategic Management Journal
27,664	8,076	3.43	Social Forces
23,448	877	26.74	Organizational Behavior and Human Performance
23,374	9,393	2.49	Harvard Business Review
22,498	1,717	13.1	Journal of Vocational Behavior
22,384	5,150	4.35	Perspectives in Psychology
20,594	2,502	8.23	Human Relations
17,836	1,116	15.98	Organizational Behavior and Human Decisions
14,596	5,132	2.84	Industrial Labor Relations Review
14,256	1,566	9.1	Journal Human Resources
12,022	1,321	9.1	Journal of Conflict Resolution
11,658	875	13.32	Journal of Management
9,082	1,185	7.66	Journal of International Business Studies
8,144	2,257	3.61	Journal of Management Studies
8,028	1,822	4.41	California Management Review
8,012	930	8.62	Journal of Occupational Psychology
7,846	904	8.68	Decision Sciences
7,221	1,868	3.87	Sloan Management Review
7,050	1,534	4.6	Industrial Relations
7,021	868	8.09	Journal of Organizational Behavior
5,633	1,598	3.53	Journal of Business Research
5,398	7,600	0.71	Monthly Labor Review
5,259	1,155	4.55	Journal of Applied Behavior Science
5,015	140	35.82	Research in Organizational Behavior
4,755	3,491	1.36	Long Range Planning
3,669	789	4.65	Organizational Dynamics
2,262	738	3.07	Administration Society
1,390	2,304	0.6	Labor Law Journal
757	693	1.09	Journal of Collective Negotiations in the Public Sector
590	1,114	0.53	Arbitration Journal

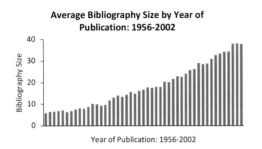
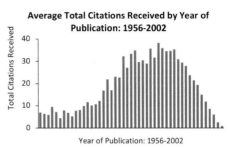

Figures 3.4a and 3.4b   *Average bibliography size by year (left) and average total citations received by year (right)*

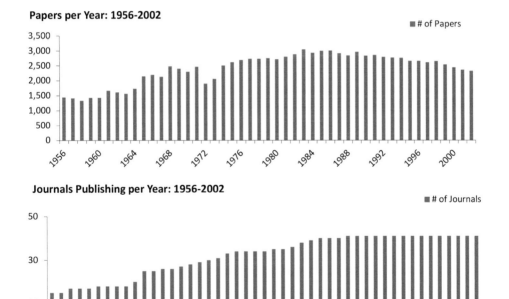

Figure 3.5   *Papers per year (top) and journals published or covered by data-source in that year (bottom)*

Diversity of Publications—In order to find a proxy for an author's more general tendency to seek a diversity of knowledge and viewpoints, we counted the number of clusters in which an author has published throughout our dataset. This provided an estimate of an author's tendency to stay in a knowledge community or move between knowledge communities. We used an entropy or diversity measure, defined as:

$$H = -\sum_{i=1}^{20} [p_i \cdot \ln(p_i)]$$

where p is the probability of being in state i. For papers with multiple authors we averaged their diversity measures.

Total Number of Papers Published—We counted an author's total number of publications, which is potentially correlated with the *Diversity of Publications* measure. For papers with multiple authors, we summed their publication counts (Table 3.3).

Table 3.3   Correlation table and descriptive statistics

		1	2	3	4	5	6	7
1	*Total Citations*	–						
2	*Bibliography Size*	0.3013*	–					
3	*CoAuthorship (binary)*	0.1443*	0.3228*	–				
4	*Cluster (binary)*	0.1460*	0.3930*	0.3590*	–			
5	*Distance*	0.1803*	0.4070*	0.3634*	0.7347*	–		
6	*Distance Squared*	0.1308*	0.2889*	0.2655*	0.5433*	0.9137*	–	
7	*Diversity*	0.1232*	0.1773*	0.3455*	0.3079*	0.3217*	0.2403*	–
	Mean	13.619	20.855	0.340	0.436	0.161	0.052	0.751
	S.D.	52.292	31 .077	0.474	0.496	0.161	0.093	0.550
	Min	0	0	0	0	0.001	0	0
	Max	4580	801	1	1	1 .480	2.190	2.453

Notes: Descriptive Statistics (n = 113,014).
* Denotes significance at the α = .05 level using the Bonferroni correction for multiple pairwise tests.

ANALYSIS AND RESULTS

Regressions

Once we identified an appropriate clustering methodology to find knowledge communities in the management literature and developed our hypotheses, we tested them using statistical regression. If our hypotheses were supported, there would be reason to believe that the individual incentive structure and the general knowledge community logic we found in an earlier chapter are consistent—that we can integrate from the micro to the macro.

In this case, the data used for our analyses were non-negative counts of the number of forward citations for papers published in 41 journals, covering both micro and macro management (sometimes called organizational behavior and strategy, respectively). As with previous measures (Morris & Moore, 2000; Ramos-Rodriguez & Ruiz-Navarro, 2004; Small & Crane, 1979) of publication citation counts, the data exhibited a variance in the number of citations larger than would be expected from a Poisson distribution. We considered using a simple negative binomial (NB) model to account for the excess variance (Hausman, Hall, & Griliches, 1984); however, the numerous zero counts in our data further indicated that a zero-inflated negative binomial regression (ZINBR) model would outperform the NB model (Figure 3.6). The use of two-stage ZINBR models is helpful when there may be a distinct process influencing the occurrence of a proportion of data points with the value of zero.[2]

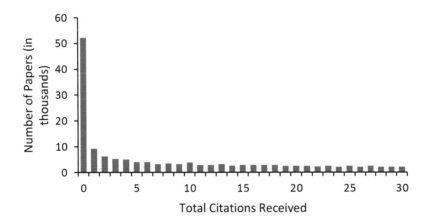

Note: Distribution of papers by number of citations shows the extreme dispersion of the data on the right, implying a negative binomial model, and the large number of zero citations on the left suggest that a zero-inflated model should be used. We cut the data off at 30 to ensure the trend was visible. Excluded papers had a total number of citation ranging up to 4,580.

Figure 3.6   Histogram of total citations received

To statistically verify our intuition-based model selection, we formally tested for over-dispersion with a Likelihood Ratio test and for excess zero counts with a Vuong test. The results confirmed that the ZINBR was the best model for our data. To further account for possible uncaptured heteroskedasticity in our models, we reported significance using Huber–White standard errors.

Models

Formally, our model is defined as:

$$\Pr(y=0) = p + (1-p)\left(1+\frac{\lambda}{\alpha}\right)^{-\alpha}$$

$$\Pr(y>0) = (1-p)\frac{\Gamma(y+\alpha)}{y!\,\Gamma(\alpha)}\left(1+\frac{\lambda}{\alpha}\right)^{-\alpha}\left(1+\frac{\alpha}{\lambda}\right)^{-y}$$

where p, the probability of a structural zero count, and λ are modeled as:

$$\ln\left(\frac{p}{1-p}\right) = c_p + a_1 v_1 + a_2 v_2 + \langle \quad \text{(the zero-inflation portion of the model)}$$

$$\ln(\lambda) = c_\lambda + b_1 w_1 + b_2 w_2 + \langle$$

where v and w are independent variables, a and b are the corresponding regression coefficients, and the cs are regression constants (intercepts). Here v and w are labeled differently, though they coincide in our models. The over-dispersion parameter $\langle$ is determined by the iterative maximum-likelihood procedure used to fit the model.

Thus, the predicted mean number of citations for a paper, given its characteristics, is $\langle$ *(1−p)* [note this is independent of $\langle$]. Using our formulations for p and $\langle$ from above and taking natural logarithms, this becomes:

$$\ln(\lambda \cdot (1-p)) = -(c_p + a_1 v_1 + a_2 v_2 + \langle) + \ln(p) + (c_\lambda + b_1 w_1 + b_2 w_2 + \langle)$$

$$\lambda \cdot (1-p) = \frac{\exp(c_\lambda + b_1 w_1 + b_2 w_2 + \langle)}{1 + \exp(c_p + a_1 v_1 + a_2 v_2 + \langle)}$$

This formulation clearly displays the difficulty of interpreting the final regression coefficients. The predicted number of citations depends on the coefficients in both the zero-inflated section and the NB section. However, the coefficients do not function in a simple additive manner. To attempt to illustrate the effect sizes of the coefficients, we utilized marginal effects plots to convey the average influence that our explanatory variables exerted in the ZINBR model. The zero-inflated portion of the model should be interpreted as predicting the likelihood of a zero count; thus, a negative coefficient in this portion indicates a decreased probability of having zero citations. The NB portion of the model can be interpreted in the usual statistical manner. Thus we would expect strongly significant predictors to exhibit opposite signs in the two portions of the ZINB model.

To capture as much of the variance in paper citations as possible before asking (and testing) our hypotheses, we created a Base Model that predicts a paper's total citations based on external paper and field characteristics, without including any cluster-specific information. For the Base Model we constructed a ZINBR model and include bibliography size, co-authorship, journal, and year effects as our explanatory variables. The year effect is necessary because papers that are published earlier tend to have accumulated a greater number of citations. We therefore controlled for publication year with dummy variables. In predicting the inflated zero counts, we utilized these same explanatory variables.

In Model I, we built upon our Base Model to explore hypothesis 7, which asked whether a paper benefits from membership to a cluster. To this end, we augmented our Base Model with the binary cluster membership variable, identifying whether or not a paper belongs to a cluster.

Model II investigates hypothesis 8, which asked whether a paper at the semi-periphery of its cluster is more likely to be highly cited. In addition to the Base Model, we included in the analysis the variable's distance from center and the squared term of distance from center. We used splines to fully characterize any nonlinear trends. Papers that were not in a cluster were excluded from consideration when fitting this model, since they have no meaningful measure for distance. Consequently, the binary cluster membership variable used in Model I was not included in this model.

For Model III, we adjusted Model I to account for the extent to which an author is benefited or harmed by publishing in many knowledge communities (represented by clusters) throughout their career. We aimed to determine whether individual papers receive more citations if the author has a diverse experience with multiple knowledge communities or within few knowledge communities in our data—a proxy for an author's more general exploratory tendencies. To do this, we included in the analysis a diversity measure to capture author publication diversity in addition to the independent variables included in Model I.

RESULTS

Our Base Model revealed that we have constructed a sound basis for modeling the number of citations received by papers (Figure 3.7). The coefficients for all independent variables were significant ($p < 0.001$) in both the zero-inflation and NB portions of the model, as shown in Table 3.4. To test the effects of our combined year and combined journal dummy variables, we fitted reduced models, eliminating each group of dummy variables in turn, and compared these models to our full models using Likelihood Ratio tests. The results of these tests confirmed our expectations that both journal of publication and year of publication were significant predictors for all of our models. The results for these tests are given in Table 3.4.

The addition of an indicator for cluster membership in Model I allows us to test whether belonging to a cluster has a positive or negative effect on a paper's total number of citations. Our Model I (Table 3.4) included significant coefficients for cluster membership in both portions, fully supporting hypothesis 7. Cluster membership, on average, was associated with receiving 15.03 more citations,[3] holding all other variables unchanged. Figure 3.8 is a visual representation of the average effect for cluster membership, as seen by the positive slope of the linear fit.

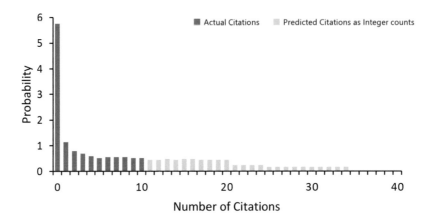

Note: This histogram allows us to compare the fit of our Base Model with the actual citation counts. In order to make the graph readable we have limited the scale to papers with 33 citations (both actual and predicted).

Figure 3.7   Histogram of total citations and base model predicted citations

As seen in Table 3.4, the independent variables from our Base Model remained significant, and the directions of these coefficients, along with their interpretations, remained the same. Furthermore, there was a strong (inverse) relationship (p <0.0001) between membership in a cluster and receiving zero citations, as seen in Table 3.5.

When computing Model II, we excluded from consideration all papers that were not assigned to a cluster (since they have no meaningful distance measure) and used a normalized measure of distance for papers that were within a cluster, ranging from 0.0 (very central) to 1.0 (extreme periphery). Model II included our variable representing distance, allowing us to test hypothesis 8. Within the NB portion of the model, the significant coefficients for distance squared and for distance indicated a potentially curvilinear relationship between distance and total citations. Within the zero-inflation portion of the model, we found that both distance and distance squared were non-significant. As seen in Figure 3.9, increasing distance from the core of a cluster was beneficial until distance reaches 0.54, and, beyond this, further increase in distance was associated with relatively fewer expected citations. Based on Model II, moving away from the optimal point in the semi-periphery by $\pm\sigma$ (S.D. = 0.1607), the number of expected citations decreased by 2.88, holding other variables constant.[4] The variables held over from our Base Model retained significance in the same direction, leaving their interpretations unchanged.

To further characterize the relationship between distance and total citations, particularly because of the skewed nature of papers toward the core of the cluster, we used linear splines to track the effects of distance over smaller intervals. As shown in Figure 3.9, the quadratic curve was a reasonable parameterization of the relationship, though the spline had a plateau in the semi-periphery rather than a clear apex.[5]

Table 3.4   *Table of coefficients*

	Negative Binomial Model Coefficients			
	Base	**I**	**II**	**III**
Cluster (binary)		0.253 ***		0.192 ***
Distance			2.743 ***	
Distance Squared			−2.439 ***	
Diversity of Sources				0.181 ***
Diversity Squared				−0.148 ***
Year of Publication	*sig.* ***	*sig.* ***	*sig.* ***	*sig.* ***
Journal Dummies	*sig.* ***	*sig.* ***	*sig.* ***	*sig.* ***
Bibliography Size	0.013 ***	0.013 ***	0.010 ***	0.012 ***
CoAuthorship (Binary)	0.193 ***	0.194 ***	0.116 ***	0.035 ***
Cluster Sum				0.009 ***
Constant	2.029 ***	1.851 ***	1.789 ***	1.515 ***
Alpha	1.449	1.436	1.234	1.388
Log-likelihood	255,172	254,773	−169,004	−253,487
Number Observations	113,014	113,014	60,840	113,014
	Zero Inflated Model Coefficients (likelihood of zero count)			
	Base	**I**	**II**	**III**
Cluster (binary)		−0.756 ***		−0.723 ***
Distance			−0.541	
Distance Squared			−0.415	
Diversity of Sources				−0.644 ***
Diversity Squared				−0.059
Year of Publication	*sig.* ***	*sig.* ***	*sig.* ***	*sig.* ***
Journal Dummies	*sig.* ***	*sig.* ***	*sig.* ***	*sig.* ***
Bibliography Size	−0.590 ***	−0.538 ***	−0.335 ***	−0.504 ***
CoAuthorship (Binary)	−1.650 ***	−1.621 ***	−1.416 ***	−1.688 ***
Cluster Sum				0.020 ***
Constant	3.266 ***	3.314 ***	2.369 ***	3.281 ***
Number Zero Observations	54,250	54,250	14,033	54,250

Notes: Coefficients and significance values for zero inflated negative binomial models.
$*p = .05$; $**p = .01$; $***p = .001$; *sig.* = significant; n.s. = not significant (significance implied by robust standard errors).
Significance reported for *Year of Publication* and *Journal Dummies* was calculated by a full vs. reduced model LR comparison test.

Model III allowed us to examine diversity of publications as a predictor of total citations. The initial results support our first competing hypothesis, which argues that a diverse publication pattern does indeed lead to more citations. Results were significant (p <0.01) for both the NB and zero-inflation portions of Model III. The positive coefficient in the NB portion indicates that increased diversity in an author's publication pattern, which is associated with the author's interaction with very diverse knowledge and perspectives, is associated with higher citation counts. Similarly, in the zero-inflation portion, the more diverse an author's citation pattern, the less likely they are to receive zero citations, as indicated by the negative coefficient. As shown in Figure 3.10, on average, an increase in diversity by one standard deviation (approximately 0.55) is associated with 6.31 additional citations, holding all other variables constant. In the robustness section, we examined this finding more closely, finding some conflicting evidence.

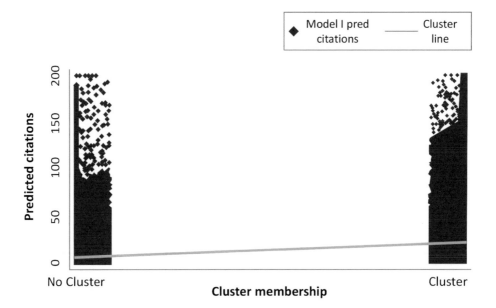

Figure 3.8   *Model I predicted citations vs. cluster membership*

Table 3.5   *Cluster membership vs. citations*

Cluster Membership vs. Zero Citations			
	Cluster Membership		
Total Citations	No	Yes	Totals
zero citations	44,618	9,631	54,249
>=1 citations	19,098	39,667	58, 765
Totals	63,716	49,298	113,014

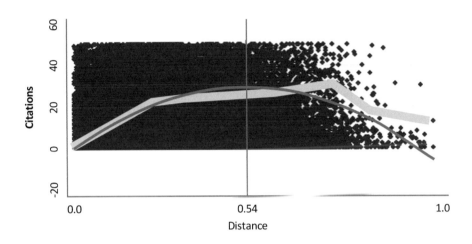

Figure 3.9   Optimal distance from core of cluster

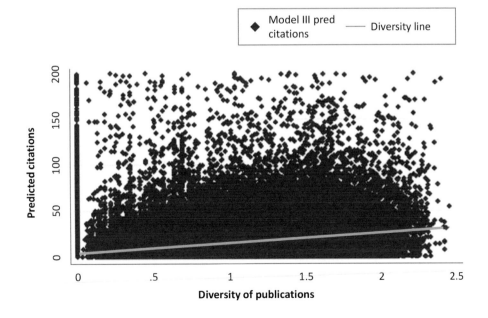

Figure 3.10   Model III predicted citations vs. diversity

ROBUSTNESS

Next, we examined several limitations in the above analysis and attempted to strengthen our findings. First, we looked more closely at our second hypothesis and explored whether the increased impact of knowledge in the semi-periphery was due to increased citations from within the knowledge community or increased attention from outside the knowledge community. Since we predicted that distance has a curvilinear relationship with total citations ranging from the core to the periphery, we split our papers into two groups—*core to semi-periphery* and *semi-periphery to periphery*—based on the distance trend noted in Figure 3.11 by dividing the data above and below the optimal distance point of the quadratic.

For each of these two parts of the data, we replaced the dependent variable in Model II with the number of citations for that paper originating from outside its cluster and from within its cluster, alternately.[6] We proceeded to test whether changes in distance led to changes in citations originating outside the cluster, which would support our theory that drawing from knowledge outside the cluster tends to lead to greater impact on knowledge outside the cluster. This new model confirmed that, for the areas of the cluster from the core to the semi-periphery, increasing distance from the core attracted significantly more out-of-cluster citations, and from the semi-periphery to the periphery, increasing distance from the core attracted fewer out-of-cluster citations.

Utilizing the peaks to either side of the central plateau identified with our splines (d = 0.3 and 0.7), we tested whether changes in distance led to changes in the number of citations from the same cluster; as before, we predicted a positive change from the core to the apex of the curve and a negative change from the midpoint to the periphery. This would bolster the idea that a paper is combining new knowledge from outside the cluster with knowledge from that cluster to generate valuable contributions within its cluster. We used citations received from within cluster (*Same Cluster Citations*) as our dependent variable and found significant support for our predictions.

Within the core to semi-periphery, an increase in distance of 0.01 is, on average, associated with an increase in citations of 4.7% and 4.8% for in-cluster and out-of-cluster citations, respectively, holding all other variables unchanged. For the semi-periphery to periphery, we found that an increase in distance of 0.01 is associated, on average, with a decrease in same-cluster citations by a factor of −0.5% and outside-cluster citations of −3.8%, holding all other variables unchanged, as shown in Figure 3.11.[7]

Second, we examined more closely hypotheses 9a and 9b about the diversity of cluster experience. While we found an overall positive impact associated with diversity in our earlier analysis, we suspect that different explanatory mechanisms may be at work depending on how high-impact the authors of the new knowledge are. We differentiated between high-impact authors, for whom diversity of publications may be reflective of high-impact new knowledge generation, and low-impact authors, who may be motivated differently when publishing in many knowledge communities without garnering citations. As an exploratory analysis, we calculated an expected citation rate for each paper using the maximum of each paper's authors' average citations within our data, and used this to partition our papers by "expected citations rates," and answer our hypothesis on these portions separately.

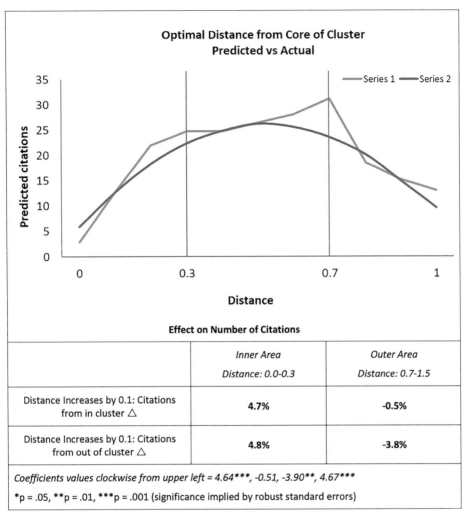

Figure 3.11 lower portion:

Effect on Number of Citations

	Inner Area *Distance: 0.0-0.3*	*Outer Area* *Distance: 0.7-1.5*
Distance Increases by 0.1: Citations from in cluster △	**4.7%**	**-0.5%**
Distance Increases by 0.1: Citations from out of cluster △	**4.8%**	**-3.8%**

Coefficients values clockwise from upper left = 4.64***, -0.51, -3.90**, 4.67***

*p = .05, **p = .01, ***p = .001 (significance implied by robust standard errors)

Notes: For regressions for the upper-right and the lower-right quadrant boxes, we used a standard negative binomial regression because the zero count was not influential enough to warrant a zero-inflated model. For the upper-left and lower-left quadrant regressions, there were substantial zero counts, so we used a zero-inflated NB model. The distance coefficient reported is only for the NB potion.

Figure 3.11   Optimal distance from core of cluster

We re-ran Model III on papers with expected citations above and below the median and in the top decile. We found similar results with respect to both direction and significance for diversity of publications among the papers, with expected citations in the lower half. For those papers with expected citations in the upper half, however, we found that an author's increasing diversity of publications was associated with a small, but significant, *decrease* in citations. This result supports our competing hypothesis 9b. We additionally ran Model III including only the top 10% of papers, based on expected citation rate. We were surprised to find that for this highest decile of papers, neither hypothesis 9a nor 9b were supported by the data. Table 3.6 gives a summary of results.[8]

Table 3.6   Author expected citations and cluster diversity

Model III – Expected Citations percentile	NB coeff. for diversity	Zero Inflation coeff. for diversity
100% (full)	0.164***	−0.719***
<50% (lower half)	−0.057*	0.453***
>50% (upper half)	0.583***	−0.273***
>90% (top ten percent)	−0.065 (n.s.)	−0.016 (n.s.)
* p < .05, *** p < .001		
Model III – Expected Citations percentile	NB coeff. for diversity	Zero Inflation coeff. for diversity
100% (full)	0.164***	−0.719***
<50% (lower half)	−0.057*	0.453***
>50% (upper half)	0.583***	−0.273***
>90% (top ten percent)	−0.065 (n.s.)	−0.016 (n.s.)
* p < .05, *** p < .001		

Overall, this section gives us added confidence in our findings for hypotheses 7 and 8, and undermines some confidence in our answer for hypothesis 9. In the section that follows, we discuss the implications and consequences of our findings.

DISCUSSION AND CONCLUSIONS

One difference between knowledge communities and formal organizations is that, because knowledge communities are generated by the behavior of their members, they are often invisible. Sometimes they have a loose label but no membership list—membership is gained through participation. They do not have formal leadership or "rules" that govern or incentivize behavior—or clearly defined goals.

In this chapter, we have drawn on theory to ask questions about the structural incentives of members of a knowledge community in the hope we could derive "group logic" from the ground up. We hoped, and found, that these communities did indeed have a logic and that their logic did, at least partly, explain why they looked the way they did. By drawing on positioning and search theory, identifying a dataset of researchers, and testing key hypotheses in that dataset, we have substantiated the idea that researchers have strong incentives to position themselves between and within knowledge communities or schools of thought, but this does not necessarily imply that authors are fully aware of this reward structure. Nor does it imply that an author who was aware of this structure could increase their impact by purposefully repositioning their citation structure or knowledge base.

Indeed, in our discussions with leading researchers in the field of management, we found that authors are generally aware of, and think about themselves in relation to, knowledge communities—though we also find that the individual descriptions of such knowledge communities, while on average close to our clusterings, vary, particularly when addressing subtle positioning choices.[9] We believe the mechanisms that explain our implicit incentive structures within and between knowledge communities are largely driven by implicit and cognitive forces rather than conscious and purposeful ones. By shaping world view, knowledge communities can powerfully affect the development of knowledge creation without explicit fiat or governance mechanisms.

The incentive structures on the individual micro-level cascade to have powerful and systematic effects on the development of a field over time. Understanding which knowledge contributions tend to get attention and have impact is crucial to understanding how a field dynamically evolves and develops.

Functionally, knowledge communities provide "small world" advantages to the process of knowledge development. Knowledge communities provide the local dense connection networks that lend themselves to learning and reputation. At the same time, the incentives toward semi-periphery positioning encourage knowledge community boundary-spanning. Our findings nicely reinforce the small world findings in the arena of knowledge creation and provide a new perspective on, and additional explanatory analysis of, the social and intellectual underpinnings of this process in the knowledge creation context.

Our results agree with the broader research, which argues that knowledge creation occurs through a moderated combination of exploration and exploitation. While we support the basic premises of positioning theory, we take into consideration previously ignored key social dimensions of intellectual positioning. We provide and analyze new boundaries for the analysis of exploration. We build on previous research that delineated knowledge communities by looking at new knowledge creation from the author-level positioning perspective. In doing so, we quantitatively tested, for the first time, the actual benefits of membership and position within a knowledge community at time of publication for a creator of new knowledge.

More generally, this chapter explored the consequences of social organization on cooperative knowledge creation. We believe that this sort of knowledge creation, where new knowledge developers share knowledge and coalesce into cohesive and distinct intellectual and social groups, is crucial in developing new knowledge. We created a quantitative framework for analyzing the positioning incentive structure that, when aggregated across all papers, shapes how knowledge develops.

We speculate that the robust incentive structures we found in clusters are maintained through selection forces within the knowledge environment. Incipient clusters that encourage too much exploration lose their integrity and fail to develop strong internal paradigms, while incipient clusters that are too internally focused may not attract sufficient attention or become too stagnant to gain momentum. Clusters that balance these two extremes in the way we describe survived to populate our dataset.

By applying performance measures to positioning in and around knowledge communities, we revealed that where knowledge is positioned has a significant impact on its performance. Indeed, by studying a complete set of articles in the top 41 journals in the social science field of micro and macro management, we found that new knowledge, which is positioned within a knowledge community can expect to get, on average, 15.03 more citations. Within a knowledge community, knowledge positioned in the semi-periphery of a knowledge community (representing knowledge that builds on a mix of knowledge common and unusual in that knowledge community), rather than at its center or periphery, results in 2.88 additional citations (± 1 S.D.).

We emphasize the complexity of new knowledge positioning because we see the act of new knowledge development as a deeply socially structured process. Knowledge communities represent more than a post hoc artifact of ideas, but rather a dynamic and important force in the future creation and knowledge landscape. This view is in keeping with the findings of researchers who show that firms that both explore and exploit in specific ways over time tend to outperform firms that do not (Gittelman, 2003; Nerkar, 2003; Rosenkopf & Nerkar, 2001).

The logic of knowledge positioning applies to R&D and science more generally. We re-ran this analysis on an extensive dataset of publications in computer science from 1992 to 2003 and found nearly identical results. Knowledge positioning will be potentially important in any field where a community of researchers exists with relatively free flows of information, inter-dependent research, and interconnected rewards—including the hard sciences and technology, where both papers and patents could be used as the unit of analysis.[10] Indeed, knowledge communities, the theoretical prerequisite for our positioning analysis, have already been identified in virtually all fields in science and technology (Aharonson et al., 2004; Braam et al., 1991a, 1991b; McCain, 1987). It remains an open question, however, how sensitive the dynamics of knowledge communities in these fields are to their differing knowledge-sharing norms and reward structure. More generally, our findings potentially offer a micro-theory that may be aggregated to offer macro-level insights into the development of research fields in science, social science, and technology in general. Studying these questions is the direction of our continued research.

Our goal in this section was to better understand the consequences of implicit and explicit positioning of researchers between and among knowledge communities. Such positioning problems are, by their nature, complex and multi-dimensional. We developed a strategic framework for analyzing how new knowledge is positioned within the knowledge landscape, considering seriously the social structure of that landscape—specifically the powerful effects of knowledge communities. We found that new knowledge was positioned by its creators under the stress of two search tensions—being a part of an identifiable knowledge community and simultaneously reaching beyond that knowledge community to draw on outside knowledge.

There are powerful advantages and subtle disadvantages provided by homophilous social groups, or knowledge communities, in the process of knowledge creation. While such knowledge communities, which represent mini-paradigms or world views, provide an audience and an intellectual structure to build on, we find that authors must also, in moderation, resist their pull and reach out beyond them to introduce fresh ideas and to appeal to outside audiences. This tension between gaining the advantages of joining a knowledge community and at the same time resisting homogenization from that knowledge community is a significant challenge for new knowledge developers while searching for new ideas, and an important part of the dynamic evolution and development of new knowledge.

COMPARATIVE ANALYSIS

Our research results strongly support our hypotheses in both Chapter 2, where we use computer science data, and in this chapter, where we use management strategy data. In each case, we applied a different statistical technique to answer the hypothesis posed. We wished to apply the analytical techniques from this chapter to the previous one, and vice versa, to see if the results hold. While this required constructing the relevant variables where they didn't already exist, because of the similarity of our underlying data structure in this and the previous chapter, we could use the data from each chapter to test the hypotheses of the other. If our conclusions are supported, this would give us additional confidence in our results and provide additional insights into the subject of this book.

In order to accomplish this "flip" of hypothesis, we first disaggregated the data used in Chapter 2 from a cluster-level analysis into a paper-level analysis. In this chapter, we used zero-inflated negative binomial regressions to test the data from the field of management strategy from 1965 to 2002. We tested how knowledge positioned itself within and between schools of thought, as well as whether knowledge producers benefited from their participation in multiple schools of thought. We were able to use the data from this chapter, which looked at the field of computer science from 1992 to 2003, to test these hypotheses again. As before, the data had a disproportionately high number of zero counts for total citations, our dependent variable. Additionally, the data exhibited over-dispersion. Following the same formal testing procedures mentioned in the primary analyses, we confirmed that the ZINBR was the proper regression technique for this scenario.

We were generally able to reconstruct similar control variables, though these data were in some ways different from the management data, resulting in subtle differences in our model constructions. The computer science data were drawn from thousands of journals and conferences, rather than a fixed 41 academic journals as with the management data. Furthermore, only some of the articles had journal or conference information because of limitations in our data source—despite our attempt to make this variable more reliable by getting additional data from the DBLP Computer Science Bibliography. For the original analysis in this chapter, aggregating the information on journals to see "journal coordination" and "journal prestige," a partial random sample was sufficient to differentiate between knowledge communities. But for a paper-by-paper level of analysis, since the majority of these data lack explicit journal or conference assignments, and the rest were highly dispersed among a large number of journals and conferences, they would not have contributed meaningfully to the model. We therefore excluded this control variable from our regression. As a test for the significance of this control we re-ran the original management data analysis without this control variable and found, as we expected, that the direction and significance of the other coefficients did not change.

Other necessary data, such as authors, years of publication, and bibliographies were available and sufficiently complete to use in the model. We had already clustered the data using StrEMer, so clusters and distance measures were available. All other variables were generated using these component variables.

Some important differences in the two databases included size, scope, and year range. The year range for the computer science data (1992–2003) was shorter, but this imposed no problem for our analysis. Indeed, as a robustness check to isolate our expected results, we re-ran the same analysis on our original management data using only papers from the same time span (1992–2003), and received the same results in direction and significance for all variables of interest. There were more papers in the computer science database than the management database, but we did not expect this to generate any difficulties. Lastly, the scope of the computer science data was more comprehensive than the original management database. In the original database we selected the top 41 journals, using a careful methodology for prestige, from among hundreds of management journals. For the computer science database, we took a much greater percentage of the total output of the field, over a shorter span of time. Therefore, we expected our results to resolve the concern we had in our original dataset when we used a sub-sample of extant data. Furthermore, since CiteSeer, the database from which the computer science data came, gathered papers from conferences, the Internet, and journals, we were also more confident that the data sample would suffer less potential bias imposed by the norms of the small group of editors in the handful of journals comprising our management data (though we have no evidence that any such bias exists). On the other hand, the computer science data were less complete for almost all variables.

Table 3.7a   Cluster-level analysis of management data, time series GLS estimation

	(1)	(2)	(3)	(4)	(5)
Cohesiveness					
Knowledge		(77.474) ***			(85.378) ***
Rhetoric		(18.266)			(19.505)
Uniqueness					
Knowledge			270.871 *		196.290
Rhetoric			13.806 $^+$		14.585
Adaptability					
Knowledge				20.559 *	15.650 *
Rhetoric				(9.731) *	(8.750) *
Control Variables					
Leadership Controls					
Journal Leadership	2.651 *	20.079 ***	2.821	6.303	24.061 ***
School Leadership	(4.282)	13.506 *	(9.464) $^+$	(7.941)	8.478
Member Leadership	(0.033)	(0.020)	(0.022)	(0.054) $^+$	(0.018)
Prestige Controls					
Journal Prestige	(1.558) ***	(1.552) ***	(1.437) ***	(1.363) ***	(1.358) ***
School Prestige	(1.248) ***	(1.022) ***	(1.077) ***	(1.303) ***	(0.886) ***
Constant	61.548 ***	56.907 ***	54.984 ***	59.132 ***	50.064 ***
N	164.000	164.000	164.000	149.000	149.000
R-squared	0.728	0.755	0.735	0.771	0.793
Chi-2	563.338	611.873	633.829	670.759	617.859

Notes: Dependent variable: number of papers published by a community in a given year.
*** $p < 0.001$; ** $p < 0.01$; * $p < 0.05$; $^+$ $p < 0.10$. Standard errors in parentheses.
Number of papers divided by 1,000 to adjust scale.

Originally, in Chapter 2, Hypotheses 1 and 2 were strongly supported, and the evidence in the third competing hypothesis led to moderated support for each hypothesis. In this chapter, our hypotheses were supported strongly over different model choices and error structures.

Table 3.7b   Cluster-level analysis of CS data [from main analysis], time series GLS estimation

	(1)	(2)	(3)	(4)	(5)
Cohesiveness					
Knowledge		(1.090) **			(1.032) **
Rhetoric		1.155 *			1.169 **
Uniqueness					
Knowledge			(4.354) *		(4.040) *
Rhetoric			1.536 ***		1.494 ***
Adaptability					
Knowledge				0.173	0.293 *
Rhetoric				(0.004)	(0.272) *
Control Variables					
Lagged Response					
One Year	0.669 ***	0.632 ***	0.591 ***	0.623 ***	0.557 ***
Leadership Controls					
Journal Leadership	(4.715) *	(4.649) *	(3.323)	(4.809) *	(3.240)
School Leadership	0.316 +	0.152	(0.249)	0.213	(0.394)
Member Leadership	(0.006) **	(0.004) +	(0.005) *	(0.005) *	(0.004) *
Prestige Controls					
Journal Prestige	0.006	0.006	(0.001)	0.005	(0.002)
School Prestige	(0.018) **	(0.018) **	(0.018) ***	(0.017) **	(0.019) ***
Member Prestige	0.004	0.004	0.010 *	0.005	0.011 **
Industry/Academy Affiliation Controls					
Pure Industry Affiliation	1.528 ***	1.454 ***	0.519 +	1.428 ***	0. 599 *
Mixed Industry/ Academy Affiliation	(0.340)	(0.518)	(0.823)	(0.508)	(0.858) +
Constant	0.176 **	0.164 **	0.103	0.149 *	0.108
N	231.000	231.000	231.000	231.000	231.000
R-squared	0.794	0.800	0.828	0.798	0.835
Chi-2	1,536.359	1,689.914	2,110.959	1,682.826	2,213.746

Notes: Dependent variable: number of papers published by a community in a given year.
*** $p < 0.001$; ** $p < 0.01$; * $p < 0.05$; + $p < 0.10$. Standard errors in parentheses.
Number of papers divided by 1,000 to adjust scale.

Table 3.8a   *Paper-level analysis of CS data*

	Negative Binomial Model Coefficients			
	Base	**1**	**2**	**3**
Cluster (binary)		0.53725282 ***		0.23419415 ***
Distance			3.0803383 ***	
Distance Squared			−3.5270229 ***	
Diversity of Sources				0.5262082 ***
Diversity of Sources Squared				−0.25267432 ***
Year of Publication Dummies	*sig.* ***	*sig.* ***	*sig.* ***	*sig.* ***
Bibliography Size	0.06281535 ***	0.04527503 ***	0.04019525 ***	0.03256502 ***
CoAuthorship (Binary)	0.16155217 ***	0.14941234 ***	0.1431387 ***	−0.09564125 ***
Pure Industry Affiliation	0.13185832 ***	0.09865867 ***	0.13147059 ***	0.15292845 ***
Mixed Academy/Industry Affiliation	0.12227623 ***	0.11112671***	0.12518428 ***	0.07983734 **
Cluster Sum				0.0068159 ***
Constant	1.0209197 ***	0.85279826 ***	1.1692341 ***	0.95557679 ***
Log (Alpha)	1.3670549 ***	1.3477003 ***	1.3530365 ***	1.3378308 ***
Log-likelihood	−430,614.55	−429,260.46	−388,101.63	−347,677.76
Number Observations	190,982	190,982	164,980	144,909
	Zero Inflated Model Coefficients (likelihood of zero count)			
	Base	**1**	**2**	**3**
Cluster (binary)		0.52929328 ***		1.5168509 ***
Distance			6.4960681 ***	
Distance Squared			−9.4561603 ***	
Diversity of Sources				0.29261587
Diversity of Sources Squared				−0.17094858
Year of Publication Dummies	*sig.* ***	*sig.* ***	*sig.* ***	*sig.* ***
Bibliography Size	−0.92349163 ***	−0.78008703 ***	−0.61839222 ***	−0.56105788 ***
CoAuthorship (Binary)	−0.49948361 ***	−0.51210551 ***	−0.5881202 ***	−0.02528598
Pure Industry Affiliation	0.51170133 ***	0.45184444 ***	0.40117791 **	0.35631596 +
Mixed Academy/Industry Affiliation	0.39787305 **	0.35372947 *	0.39342381 *	0.54185649 *
Cluster Sum				−0.12038881 **
Constant	−0.59272862 ***	−1.0063603 ***	−1.2821031 ***	−2.0283008 ***
Number Zero Observations	91,188	91,188	75,923	65,353

Notes: Coefficients and significance values for zero inflated negative binomial models.
$^{+}p = 0.10$; $^{*}p = .05$; $^{**}p = .01$; $^{***}p = .001$; *sig.* = significant; *n.s.* = not significant; (significance implied by robust standard errors).
Significance reported for Year of Publication Dummies was calculated by a full vs reduced model LR comparison test.

Table 3.8b   Paper-level analysis of management data [from main analysis]

Negative Binomial Model Coefficients				
	Base	**1**	**2**	**3**
Cluster (binary)		0.253 ***		0.192 ***
Distance			2.743 ***	
Distance Squared			−2.439 ***	
Diversity of Sources				0.181 ***
Diversity Squared				−0.148 ***
Year of Publication	*sig.* ***	*sig.* ***	*sig.* ***	*sig.* ***
Journal Dummies	*sig.* ***	*sig.* ***	*sig.* ***	*sig.* ***
Bibliography Size	0.013 ***	0.013 ***	0.010 ***	0.012 ***
CoAuthorship (Binary)	0.193 ***	0.194 ***	0.116 ***	0.035 ***
Cluster Sum				0.009 ***
Constant	2.029 ***	1.851 ***	1.789 ***	1.515 ***
Alpha	1.449	1.436	1.234	1.388
Log-likelihood	−255,172	−254,775	−169,004	253,407
Number Observations	113,014	113,014	60,840	113,014
Zero Inflated Model Coefficients (likelihood of zero count)				
	Base	**1**	**2**	**3**
Cluster (binary)		−0.756 ***		−0.723 ***
Distance			−0.541	
Distance Squared			−0.415	
Diversity of Sources				−0.644 ***
Diversity Squared				−0.059
Year of Publication	*sig.* ***	*sig.* ***	*sig.* ***	*sig.* ***
Journal Dummies	*sig.* ***	*sig.* ***	*sig.* ***	*sig.* ***
Bibliography Size	−0.590 ***	−0.538 ***	−0.335 ***	−0.504 ***
CoAuthorship (Binary)	−1.650 ***	−1.621 ***	−1.416 ***	−1.688 ***
Cluster Sum				0.020 ***
Constant	3.266 ***	3.314 ***	2.369 ***	3.281 ***
Number Zero Observations	54,250	54,250	14,033	54,250

Notes: Coefficients and significance values for zero inflated negative binomial models.
* $p = .05$; ** $p = .01$; *** $p = .001$; *sig.* = significant; *n.s.* = not significant; (significance implied by robust standard errors).
Significance reported for year of publication and Journal Dummies was calculated by a full vs reduced model LR comparison test.

In this new analysis, these models strongly confirm our original findings, perhaps even with a higher degree of statistical significance. A comparison of Table 3.7a with Table 3.7b (equivalent to Table 2.3 in our primary analysis) reveals that these coefficients are uniformly in agreement with our hypotheses. Analysis of the predicted values yields the following estimates, which mirror our original estimates. As predicted in hypothesis 7, a paper that is published in a cluster will receive, on average, 4.27 citations more than a similar paper published outside a cluster, assuming other variables in our model are unchanged. Similarly, confirming hypothesis 8, a paper at the semi-periphery will receive, on average, 1.33 citations more than a paper in the core or in the periphery—defined here by moving 2 standard deviations away from the semi-periphery—assuming all other variables remained unchanged. Lastly, confirming hypothesis 9, our model predicts that moving from the peak of the diversity curve by 2 standard deviations in either direction will yield, on average, 0.86 fewer citations. See Table 3.8a for the results of this analysis. Table 3.8b provides the original coefficients from our primary analysis for comparison.

We then took the management data and applied them to the computer science database. The program that aggregated the original data was hard coded for the years 1992–2003, so our analysis was limited to those years. We had a few concerns with data appropriateness in testing the hypotheses in this chapter. The management data were only a sub-sample of the 41 most prestigious journals in the field of management. When we were measuring paper positioning this was an advantage; we were able to see how papers were positioned in their knowledge landscape in the top journals by top scholars. But when measuring aggregate community characteristics, this is a potential detraction. The small sample size may not have been enough to capture broad community characteristics, and the journals' high prestige might not have captured the general characteristics of their communities.

In order to recapture the "journal prestige" variable, we used the ranking of journal influence in management by Podsakoff et al. (2005); for the "school prestige" variable we used the U.S. News and World Report ranking of top business programs by academic rank. We excluded author prestige, built from honors given to computer scientists by the Institute for Electrical and Electronics Engineers, the Association of Computing Machinery, and the National Academy of Engineering, because we had no analogous list of honors in management. We also excluded the time lag because a Wooldridge test for serial autocorrelation was not significant. We computed all other variables as per our original analysis.

Our results generally support our hypotheses and mirror our prior findings. In our full model, hypotheses 1, 5, and 6 are directly confirmed with statistical significance. Coefficients for hypotheses 2, 3, and 4 are not statistically significant, but two of these three are in the expected direction. Knowledge uniqueness is both not statistically significant and not in the expected direction; this is also the variable in this chapter for which we found the least support, shedding some doubt on this hypothesis and/or suggesting that the variable suffers from the same collinearity issues identified and explored in our primary analysis. Our results confirm the original finding that school prestige is negative and significant, as well as the general trend of prestige variables having negative coefficients.

NOTES

1. Reclusterings using data for five years after publication t(0) to t(5) and for the ten years around the publication t(−5) to t(5) yielded comparable similar distance measures, implying that cluster centrality changes gradually.
2. We anticipate that numerous papers will not be cited for structural reasons, including article type, journal, and bibliography characteristics. Other papers in our database received no citations for the time period covered simply due to chance. There are also papers that are cited frequently, leading to over-dispersion in our dataset.

3. 15.03 is the slope of the line plotted in Figure 3.6. It is the difference between predicted citation counts for in-cluster papers and non-cluster papers after removing extreme outliers.

4. 2.88 is the difference in Model II between predicted citations at distance = 0.54 and ±1 S.D. (distance ≈ .36 or distance ≈ 0.68).

5. Given the mechanism of our clustering algorithm, there could be different reasons for a paper to be on the semi-periphery of a cluster. Papers with high impact could be on the semi-periphery because they cite unusual papers, either inside or outside their own cluster, or because they cite a mix of papers both within and outside their cluster. To explore the drivers of semi-peripheral placement for high-impact papers, we constructed two additional variables to capture the average distance of each paper's citations within and outside its cluster and added both these variables into our model for hypothesis 8. We found that the coefficients for both these variables were positive and highly significant, implying that successful papers in the semi-periphery tended to cite a mix of central papers, both within cluster and in central papers within other clusters.

    We hypothesized that a paper that combined knowledge from its own cluster with a few—perhaps one or two—outside clusters, rather than many outside clusters, would be the most successful. This would allow it to act as a bridge between a few audiences or research communities. To test this, we constructed, for each paper, a Herfindahl Index of cluster concentration for citations made to a paper within another cluster. We did this by summing, for each paper with more than four outside citations, the percentage of citations to papers in each outside cluster. A higher Herfindahl cluster concentration score would imply that the paper made a high percentage of outside citations to one cluster; a lower Herfindahl score would imply that a paper scattered its outside citations to many papers. We added this variable for concentration into the regression for Model II, and it was positive and highly significant. This confirms the intuition that papers that bring together knowledge from a few schools of thought tend to be well cited.

6. For two of these four models, there were too few papers with zero citations to justify a zero-inflated model, and the standard NB model produced a sufficiently accurate fit for this analysis. Thus, for these two models, we used a negative binomial regression (see Figure 3.9).

7. In this case the percentage change in citations is equal to $\exp(\circledR * ^{TM})$, where ^{TM} is the incremental change in which you are interested and $\circledR$ represents the respective coefficient in the model (Long, 1997).

8. We sought to confirm that our clustering algorithm identifies meaningful schools of thought. While it compares favorably to other algorithms of its kind, we wanted to separately test whether the specific tests we claim remained significant if we randomize the cluster assignment for all papers in the same proportions that exist in our dataset, and monitor our results for any changes. Our first hypothesis asks if being in a cluster is advantageous in garnering citations; once we randomize citation assignments (and therefore cluster membership), this effect should disappear if the clusters are in fact meaningful. This would add confidence that our results are not an artifact of clustering or statistical methodology. We found that after randomizing we lost significance for our binary cluster variable, as expected. The cluster assignments were successfully randomized ($\chi^2_{(324)} = 276.0230$, $p = 0.975$). The coefficients for our new binary cluster membership variable in our model were now insignificant (NB portion: $p = 0.403$; zero-inflation portion: $p = 0.361$). These results support the validity of our clustering methodology. Lastly, we wanted to further rule out the possibility that the excess zero counts in our data obscured the true trends, despite our use of the ZINBR formulation. To accomplish this, we excluded all zero-citation papers and proceeded to refit our data with a standard Negative Binomial model. The direction and significance of our coefficients in the NB portion of our previous models remain unchanged. We do not believe that the zero-inflation portion of our model was incorrectly identifying and modeling the excess zero counts or obscuring the trend among those papers that received citations.

9. Since statistical correlation does not imply causation, an explicit positioning and, in particular, a shallow manipulation of citation structure without a change in knowledge base and search structure is unlikely to affect impact deeply.

10. Patents will differ from papers in many respects. The purpose of patents is to establish a proprietary claim on a method, idea, or technology, while the purpose of a paper is to advance knowledge and share information. Nevertheless, we believe both will exhibit interesting and useful clusters of patterns.

APPENDIX 3.1   DESCRIPTION OF CLUSTERING

Methodology[1]

Our clustering algorithm clusters items in three steps (repeated when doing iterated "overlapping" clustering). In Step I, we make a single pass over the data and construct several rough clusters. In Step II, we get a collection of high-quality clusters, called committees, based on the clusters we get in Step I. These committees are tight and differ from each other, indicating high intergroup similarity and low intra-group similarity between papers. In Step III, each element is either assigned to its most similar cluster, or added to the residue list if it is not similar enough to any cluster. We now give a more detailed description of each step.

Step I

The objective of this step is to find a collection of rough clusters over the data, from which we can form high-quality committees in Step II. For each element, we compute its similarity to the centroid of every cluster in our cluster list, which is initially empty. The centroid is the average citation structure of all papers in the cluster. We say an element is far away from all other clusters if its similarity to every existing cluster is below some similarity threshold θ_1. The algorithm then adds this element as a new singleton cluster to the cluster list. Otherwise, the element is assigned to its most similar cluster.

Step II

The second step of the clustering algorithm finds a set of committees, which are tight and well-scattered in the similarity space. The output of Step I consists of rough and low-quality clusters—clusters that might be very close to each other, and have a very small number of elements, even singletons. We call these "committee candidates." Based on those candidates, the algorithm finds as many committees as possible, on the condition that each newly discovered committee is big enough and not too similar to any existing committee.

This selection process uses the parameters "minsize" and θ_2. The parameter "minsize" in line 9 and line 12 of the pseudocode in Appendix 3.2, filters out small-size clusters, and reflects our preference for bigger committees. Each candidate is only kept as a committee if it is big enough and, more important, its similarity to every committee candidate is below some threshold for cluster cohesiveness. Cluster cohesiveness is calculated by averaging the similarity between each of its elements and its centroid:

$$\frac{\sum_{i=1}^{n_c} sim(e_i, cen_c)}{n_c}$$

where C represents a cluster; i indexes papers in cluster C; and $sim(\cdot)$ is the measure of similarity, as previously defined, and n_C is the number of papers in cluster C. Each committee that is found in this step will define one of the final output clusters of this algorithm.

Step III

The final step of the algorithm resembles the traditional clustering methodologies kmeans and CBC, in that each element is assigned to its most similar clusters. In this case, for each element, if its similarity to a committee exceeds some high similarity threshold θ_3, it is assigned to the cluster containing the committee. If an element's similarity to every cluster is below θ_3, that is, it is far away from any cluster, it is added to the list of residues.

NOTE

1. Clustering methodology was developed with Lyle Ungar.

APPENDIX 3.2   PSEUDOCODE

Input: A list of elements E to be clustered, thresholds θ_1, θ_2, and θ_3 and minimum size *minsize*.

Step 1: $C \leftarrow \{\}$; $Cen \leftarrow \{\}$
2   **for each** $e \in E$
3   **if** $sim(e,c) < \theta_1$, **for** $\forall c \in C$, **then**
4      $C \leftarrow C \cup \{\{e\}\}$
5   **else** $c' = \arg\max_{c \in C}[sim(e,c)]$
6      $c' \leftarrow c' \cup \{e\}$
7   **end if**
8   **update(** Cen **)**
9   **end for**

Step 2:
1    $new\_C \leftarrow \{\}$
2   **for each** $c \in C$
3     $cen\_v \leftarrow$ centroid vector of c
4     $num \leftarrow$ number of elements in c
5     $cohesiveSim(c) = \sum_{e \in c} sim(e, cen\_v) \big/ num$
6   **end for**
7   **for each** $c \in C$
8   **if** $sim(c,x) < \theta_2$, **for** $\forall x \in C$, **then**
9   **if** size(c) > minsize,
10       $new\_C \leftarrow new\_C \cup \{c\}$
11   **end if**
12   **else** $s \leftarrow \{x : x \in C, sim(c,x) < \theta_2 \cup size(x) > min\,size\}$
13      $c' = \arg\max_{x \in s}[cohesiveSim(x)]$
14      $new\_C \leftarrow new\_C \cup \{c'\}$
15   **end if**
16   **end for**

Step 3:
1    $L \leftarrow new\_C$; $R \leftarrow \{\}$
2   **for each** $e \in E$
3   **for each** $c \in new\_C$
4   **if** $sim(e,c) > \theta_3$, **then**
5       $l \leftarrow l \cup \{e\}, l \in L \wedge c \subseteq l$
6   **end if**
7   **end for**
8   **if** $e \notin l$, **for** $\forall l \in L$, **then**
9      $R \leftarrow R \cup \{e\}$
10   **end if**
11   **end for**

Output: A list of clusters

APPENDIX 3.3   CLUSTERS FORM AND DISBAND OVER TIME

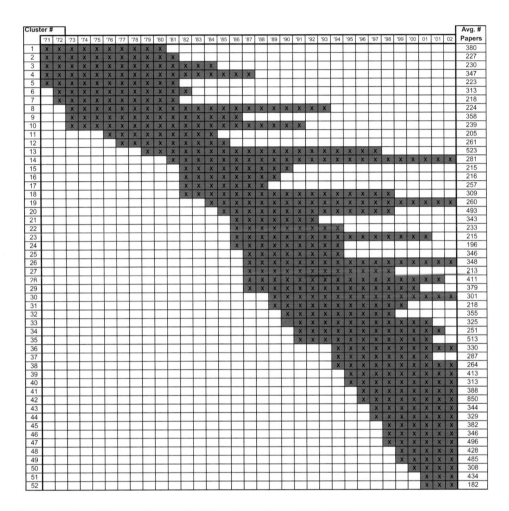

Figure 3A.1   Clusters form and disband over time, 1971–2002

4. Emerging research fronts in science and technology: identifying breakout ideas early

INTRODUCTION AND THEORY

Why do some areas of research flourish and have enormous impact, while others fade or languish in obscurity? In science and technology, this question takes on particular importance because a breakthrough can cure a disease, allow for new inventions, or help us understand the world. The areas of scientific research that generate intense interest from other scientists tend to be perceived as the most promising (Albert et al., 1991; Braam, Moed, & Vanraan, 1988; Min, Bu, & Sun, 2021), are particularly well funded (Boyack & Borner, 2003), and are more likely to result in commercial discoveries (Narin et al., 1997; Pedraza-Fariña & Whalen, 2020; Tortoriello et al., 2015; Trajtenberg, 1990). Our core interest in this work is to understand the functioning of knowledge communities—we believe understanding how these knowledge communities first form, and what allows them to take-off and succeed, will be helpful to understanding their more mature forms. We focus on the clusters of the most highly cited areas of research, called "research fronts," and provide quantitative and qualitative support for continued, focused study of these "hot" research areas as important for understanding the development of science and technology more broadly. These areas of intensive work are interesting to R&D laboratories looking for future innovation breakthroughs, venture capitalists looking to allocate investment, governments interested in promoting emerging science, and researchers hoping to work on promising topics (Niemann et al., 2017).

The long-term goal of this work is to develop a methodology for identifying and tracking highly cited research areas at the micro-specialty level as they emerge. Furthermore, it is to understand the role these fronts play in the development of science and technology, how they grow into knowledge communities, and what would help them to innovate more quickly. We wanted to use a methodology that does not presuppose the existence of any specific research area, such as would be required in a traditional literature-searching approach, nor any prior knowledge about the scientific area, but instead relies on an objective, comprehensive monitoring of attention by other experts. It should be possible to increase or decrease the sensitivity of the detection by adjusting parameters, and to utilize a marker for research areas that allows direct comparison of different time slices. In addition, the method should be multidisciplinary and utilize field normalization to obtain a systematic view across different disciplines. The scope should be scalable, from the micro-structure to the macro-structure of science, to see the context of the innovation. Finally, the method should capture both social aspects and the topical content of scientific areas.

To explore this idea quantitatively, we used the Web of Science database from Thomson Scientific of over 8,500 journals and over one million articles per year in the sciences and social sciences, and analyzed it for emerging fronts representing new micro-evolutions in science. Our data consisted of very highly cited articles clustered through co-citation to obtain cohesive sets of articles. Various studies have shown that these clusters, or fronts, represent small groups of scientists working on potentially important innovations (Small, 2018a, 2018b). Only a few studies have attempted to find or predict emerging areas of research, particularly over such a comprehensive database (Small, 2006, 2018a). We studied the validity of our methodology by interviewing scientists about the accuracy and success of our predictions. The insights gained by our qualitative interviews support the success of our method and will contribute to future attempts to identify emerging trends in research.

For research fronts that generate powerful findings there are two possible outcomes—they can grow independently as areas of study, or be "absorbed" by others through their impact. In the first case, the front may initially grow in size and then, potentially, split off as a new field of research, or even develop into a new discipline (Antons et al., 2020; Small & Greenlee, 1990). Alternatively, in the second case, a successful front may have great influence on its field and thus be incorporated by it, effectively being "absorbed" by the appropriation of the insights of the front within a broader field. This process of absorption, as it pertains to specific findings and papers in science, was described by Robert Merton as "obliteration by incorporation," in which explicit mention of prior knowledge can disappear because of its very success in generating interest and use (Merton, 1968, 1972).

In this study, we distinguished between these two outcomes by differentiating between fronts that "emerge" by growing in size (growth) and fronts that are "absorbed" as a result of their papers being increasingly cited (impact), resulting in a kind of absorption through diffusion. Which fronts emerge and which are absorbed, we hypothesize, is significant in determining the shape and structure of scientific and technical research as it evolves.

One notable aspect of research fronts is their potential to span traditional scientific disciplines. Potentially, for example, fronts that combine disciplines and challenge existing paradigms will have more difficulty being absorbed and may, in aggregate, presage paradigm shifts (Kuhn, 1962). The progress of science is a result of the virtual and actual collaboration of thousands of scientists who, formally and informally, share their findings and build on one another's work (Boyack & Borner, 2003). The research on explicit collaboration between scientists has emphasized the value of cross-company alliances, informal networks, and social capital (Gittelman, 2003). Indeed, interdisciplinary work, as a process for sharing information and, as an inspiration for analogies, is often seen as one of the drivers of innovation (Amir, 1985; Birnbaum, 1981a, 1981c; Ponzi, 2002). In the absence of such interdisciplinary work, knowledge tends to become more compartmentalized and the interference of disruptive paradigms becomes more likely, as tensions between distinct theories accumulate (Fleming & Sorenson, 2001). We examined the role of interdisciplinary research in research fronts when knowledge combines from different disciplines in an intellectually cohesive manner (Cuhls, 2003; Fleming & Sorenson, 2001).

The effort to understand innovation through an examination of co-citations among scientific and technical papers began at the Institute for Scientific Information—now Thomson Scientific—in the 1970s (Small, 1976). As Sullivan, White, and Barboni (1977) put it: "A series of claims for the technique of co-citation analysis have been made by Henry Small at ISI and collaborators. The first and most important claim is that co-citation clusters 'reflect the … cognitive structures of research specialties.'" In addition, researchers found that citation structure might be used to gain insight into the social structure of science and technology—how knowledge changes and develops over time (Crane, 1972; Garfield & Stevens, 1965; Small, 2003). That these ideas could be revealed through citation analysis was crystallized conceptually by Diana Crane (1972), based on older ideas of the social structure of science pioneered by Derek Price, Thomas Kuhn, and Robert Merton (Kuhn, 1962; Merton, 1972; Price, 1961, 1963).

Much of the earlier research in this field has focused on delineating the structure of science using algorithms that find similar papers and organize them into clusters (Small, 1977). Later studies have mapped-out specific fields, such as scientometrics itself (Chen et al., 2002), management and information science (Culnan, 1986, 1987), organizational behavior (Culnan et al., 1990), chemical engineering (Milman & Gavrilova, 1993), economics (Oromaner, 1981), and space communication (Hassan, 2003). Many researchers have subsequently focused on the visualization of these fields, developing tools such as crossmapping and DIVA (Morris & Moore, 2000), HistCite (Garfield, 1988; Garfield, Pudovkin, & Istomin, 2003), and Pathfinder (White, 2003), and methods for graphing large-scale maps of science (Small, 1997). (For a good review of the seminal literature, see Osareh, 1996).

Morris and Moore developed a method to help expert panels evaluate small research topics (Morris & Moore, 2000). This method organizes papers visually over time and studies the evolution of a topic, such as anthrax research. The focus is on temporal changes and timeline visualizations. Morris and Moore first cluster documents based on bibliographic coupling and then visualize clusters using horizontal timeline tracks, plotting documents along them. Because timeline visualizations can reveal temporal relations among research areas and their documents, timelines are potentially useful tools in identifying the convergence of distinct fields.

Henry Small developed a comprehensive method for identifying and tracking research fronts (Small, 2003), based on the co-citation of highly cited papers. We build on Small's methodology and suggest additional screens to weed-out certain artifactual clusters. We use interviews with experts in the field to evaluate how well our method identifies significant areas (also used by Braam et al., 1988) and present four case studies to explore the scope and nature of research fronts.

METHODOLOGY FOR DELINEATING RESEARCH AREA

Unlike most methods for analyzing research areas, co-citation clustering is an a priori method that makes no assumptions about what research areas exist, but rather selects whatever papers are highly cited and subjects these to a cluster analysis. This is essentially the methodology used in machine learning and data compression, applied to innovation. The basic limitation of this method is that it will not identify a specialty if no papers have become highly cited. Therefore it is expected that a co-citation method will not detect an area immediately upon its emergence, but will detect it at some stage early in its development. It should be emphasized that the method does not identify all papers that might be considered relevant to the area. Rather, it is designed to detect that an area exists and provide samples of its highly cited and citing papers. For this study, highly cited papers are defined as the top 1% of papers in each of 22 broad disciplines, as defined in InCites.

Papers are grouped into co-citation clusters through a single-link process. Single-link clustering is a simple way to extract the patterns of strong links among a set of papers, provided we used a strategy for preventing chaining. Chaining tends to act like gravity, and sucks all new ideas into powerful old ones, obscuring how novel they are. To track clusters over time, we looked at successive time slices of data to determine the patterns of continuing highly cited papers from one dataset to the next. Such patterns of continuity are referred to as cluster strings (Small & Greenlee, 1990). A new or emerging area is defined as a cluster of highly cited papers in one time period whose papers did not appear in any clusters in the immediately preceding time period.

All co-citations for the selected highly cited papers in the 22 fields were computed. In this case, a co-citation link is defined as a pair of highly cited papers, co-cited two or more times. The integer co-citation frequency was normalized by dividing it by the square root of the product of the citation counts of the two papers, the so-called cosine similarity. Clusters were defined by setting a threshold on the cosine similarity of 0.3. The single-link clustering in effect gathers together links that share common papers to form a network. To prevent chaining, a maximum cluster size of 50 was set. If the cluster exceeded this size, the cosine threshold was incremented and the link-gathering process repeated at the higher threshold. The process was continued until a cluster of size 50 or less is formed. The process is analogous to pruning a tree where none of the branches cut off are allowed to be larger than a preset size (Small & Sweeney, 1985).

Two sets of co-citation clusters were used, representing two overlapping six-year time periods: 1998–2003 and 1999–2004. Both cited and citing papers were restricted to these time spans. Papers also included some of our results from clustering earlier time periods. Table 4.1 gives statistics on the datasets used: the number of clusters, highly cited papers, average citations per paper, and average publication year of papers.

Table 4.1   Statistics on clusters in two time periods

	1998–2003	1999–2004
# Clusters	5,269	5,350
# Papers	21,315	21,411
Cites per paper	76.9	75.4
Average year	2000.6	2001.6

The field or discipline assignment of a cluster was determined by the journals in which the highly cited papers are published. The discipline weight for a cluster was defined as the number of papers in a particular discipline. As we would expect, there was a tendency for larger clusters to have larger numbers of disciplinary assignments.

In Figure 4.1, the 1999–2004 data show where papers comprising the clusters are distributed by discipline in our dataset (as a percentage of the total). The stability of most disciplines over time is notable, with the exception of an apparent slight trend upward in the biological sciences, such as molecular biology, biology, and microbiology.

One type of cluster we found with the methodology might be considered an artifact of the publishing process. It is the result of a set of papers that artificially cite each other—for example, the case of a "single issue cluster" (Rousseau & Small, 2006; Small, 2006), formed when an editor creates a special issue of a journal and arranges each article to cite some or all of the other articles in the same issue, creating a citation clique. Normally, cited and citing document populations are somewhat distinct, but in the above case potentially every citing item is also a cited item.

Because clusters are defined for a multi-year period, e.g., 1999–2004, it is possible for a highly cited paper to also legitimately function as a citing paper for the group. This would happen, for example, if a paper citing one of the founding papers in the front became itself highly cited before the end of the time period. The degree to which citing papers are also cited papers would then, conceptually, measure the extent to which the papers are building on each other. To capture this, we created a metric called endogeneity, discussed in detail later, which is the percentage of citing papers that are also cited papers. The average endogeneity for the dataset is quite low: 2.3.

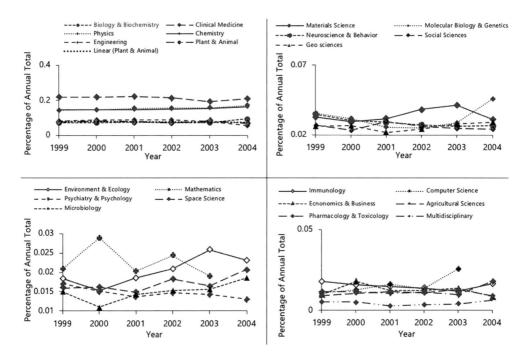

Figure 4.1   Discipline size over time

Only about 1.5% of clusters had an endogeneity percentage of 20% or higher. Most of these clusters were almost certainly an artifact of an editorial policy and did not reflect the emergence of a true new research front. Therefore, for our quantitative analysis, we have excluded any cluster having an endogeneity percentage of 20% or higher. Naturally occurring levels of moderate endogeneity, below 20%, may indeed be a healthy sign for a research area, indicating that there are highly cited papers in the current citing paper population and that the front is efficiently building on its own findings (Pfeffer, 1993).

Clustering methodology can get technical, and is sometimes confusing. But it is also extremely powerful. In theory, we are doing the same thing that Google does when it finds "similar" web pages, or that bioinformatics does when it finds related gene sequences. Once highly related clusters are identified at an early stage (and using a forward-looking technology), a whole series of statistical methods can be applied to them to see what cluster characteristics can be predictive of cluster success.

QUALITATIVE ANALYSIS

The dataset we are using to study emerging clusters in science and technology is comprehensive—it includes original research in science, much of which will result in powerful new insights and inventions. But getting useful insights from this data is the key to our efforts. Can we use clustering analysis (only looking backward) to identify meaningful clusters that are more likely to ultimately become important fields of study? If this is possible, even using crude methodology, it could result in some powerful insights. To test our success in identifying new fronts relatively early in their development, we selected a sample of 20 of the largest fronts that emerged in one of the three most recent time periods. As a first step we gathered and studied the full texts of the 360+ articles included in these clusters. The topics of each cluster are listed in Table 4.2.

Past research has typically focused on picking areas or fronts that were ex post judged to be interesting, and then tracing their history. Our method has identified these clusters, potentially before are widely recognized as important areas of research, using co-citation data alone, not reputation or word of mouth. Our objective is both to confirm that we identified the emerging fronts accurately and to validate our methodology by talking to experts in the field (Boyack & Borner, 2003; Cuhls, 2003; Falkingham & Reeves, 1998).

INTERVIEWS

To test whether the automated cluster analysis resulted in meaningful areas of emerging research, we contacted researchers in the specific research areas at the University of Pennsylvania, Drexel University, Columbia University, and New York University, USA. One of the most coherent and fastest-growing fields was organic thin-film transistors, so we conducted interviews on this topic with industry experts working in this front. In total, we interviewed 30 researchers, with interviews lasting from thirty minutes to two hours, providing them with full texts of all papers in each front.

We began by asking if this was, in their opinion, an interesting or important area of research, if it was a cohesive front, and if, in looking at the papers in the front in detail, they observed any patterns or omissions. We continued in an unstructured conversation on these topics. Previous studies that made extensive use of interviews in conjunction with citation analysis found interviews to be a crucial sense-making tool (Braam et al., 1991a, 1991b; Castro & Lima, 2001; Collins, 1997; Cuhls, 2003; Small, 1977, 2004).

The most common result from our interviews was support that our method had picked out interesting and cohesive areas in very specific sub-fields of technical research. Of these, about half the time the experts/researchers said that the program had indeed identified an emerging area in their sub-specialty, and that it was one that was not obvious until the group itself was

Table 4.2　Summary of 20 emerging clusters examined more closely

Cluster #	Name of cluster / Keywords	Disciplines	Top Cited Paper	# of Papers	Total Cites
1	PLANE WAVES	Physics	Type IIB Green-Schwarz superstring in plane wave Ramond-Ram and background	22	274
	PP-WAVE BACKGROUND: ORBIFOLDED ADS(5) X S-5; PP-WAVE LIMITS; PENROSE LIMITS				
2	AMYLOID PRECURSOR PROTEIN (APP)	Molecular Biology & Genetics, Biology & Biochemistry, Neuroscience & Behavior, Multidisciplinary	A transcriptively active complex of APP with Fe65 and histone acetyltransferase Tip60	21	467
	PRESENILIN-MEDIATED AMYLOID PRECURSOR PROTEIN CARBOXYL-TERMINAL FRAGMENT GAMMA; BETA-AMYLOID PRECURSOR PROTEIN FAMILY RESEMBLING GAMMA-SECRETASE-LIKE CLEAVAGE				
3	LARGE BLACK HOLES	Physics	Black holes and sub-millimeter dimensions	18	338
	BLACK HOLE FACTORIES: BLACK HOLES RADIATE MAINLY; HIGH ENERGY COSMIC RAY SPECTRUM: ULTRAHIGH-ENERGY COSMIC RAYS				
4	MICROFLUIDIC ANALYTICAL SYSTEMS	Chemistry, Engineering	Towards stationary phases for chromatography on a microchip	14	167
	AMINO ACIDS USING PHOTOPATTERNED RIGID POLYMER MONOLITHS; HIGH-RESOLUTION CHIRAL SEPARATION USING MICROFLUIDICS-BASED MEMBRANE CHROMATOGRAPHY; RAPID MICROFLUIDIC MIXING				
5	NOGO-66 RECEPTOR	Neuroscience & Behavior, Molecular Biology & Genetics, Biology & Biochemistry	Nogo-A is a myelin-associated neurite outgrowth inhibitor and an antigen for monoclonal antibody IN-1	14	431
	PROMOTES AXONAL REGENERATION: MYELIN-ASSOCIATED NEURITE OUTGROWTH INHIBITOR: SPINAL AXON REGENERATION INDUCED: NOGO RECEPTOR LIGAND: MYELIN-ASSOCIATED GLYCOPROTEIN (MAG)				
6	EKPYROTIC UNIVERSE	Physics	Ekpyrotic universe: Colliding branes and the origin of the hot big bang - art. no. 123522	14	178
	CYCLIC EKPYROTIC SCENARIOS; EKPYROTIC MODELS; NEW EKPYROTIC; CYCLIC UNIVERSE				
7	C-AXIS ORIENTED SUPERCONDUCTING	Physics	Optical conductivity and penetration depth in MgB2 - art. no. 097003	14	149
	C-AXIS-ORIENTED SUPERCONDUCTING MGB2 THIN FILM; MGB2 JUNCTIONS; FAR-INFRARED OPTICAL CONDUCTIVITY GAP; MULTIBAND OPTICAL PROPERTIES				

Cluster #	Name of cluster	Disciplines	Top Cited Paper	# of Papers	Total Cites
	Keywords				
8	SARS	Clinical Medicine, Microbiology, Plant & Animal Science	*Coronavirus as a possible cause of severe acute respiratory syndrome*	25	1139
	FATAL SEVERE ACUTE RESPIRATORY SYNDROME; 14 SARS CORONAVIRUS ISOLATES; NOVEL CORONAVIRUS ASSOCIATED; SARS VIRUS				
9	COPPER-FREE COUPLING	Chemistry	*Activation of aryl chlorides for Suzuki cross-coupling by ligandless, heterogeneous palladium*	23	434
	SONOGASHIRA CROSS-COUPLING REACTIONS; HIGHLY ACTIVE PALLADIUM/ACTIVATED CARBON CATALYSTS; SONOGASHIRA REACTIONS; CATALYTIC CROSS-COUPLING REACTIONS MEDIATED				
10	HUMAN SNAIL3 GENE	Clinical Medicine	*Identification and characterization of human PRICKLE1 and PRICKLE2 genes as well as mouse Prickle1 and Prickle2 genes homologous to Drosophila tissue polarity gene prickle*	23	395
	*HUMAN DAAM2 GENE; HUMAN ZPBP-LIKE GENE; HUMAN INSCUTEABLE GENE; HUMAN T*PARP GENE*				
11	ORAL DIRECT THROMBIN INHIBITOR	Clinical Medicine, Chemistry, Pharmacology & Toxicology	*The direct thrombin inhibitor melagatran and its oral prodrug H 376/95: Intestinal absorption properties, biochemical and pharmacodynamic effects*	14	379
	NOVEL ORAL DIRECT THROMBIN INHIBITOR; DIRECT THROMBIN INHIBITOR MELAGATRAN FOLLOWED; ORAL XIMELAGATRAN; TOTAL KNEE REPLACEMENT				
12	COMPREHENSIVE 2-D GAS CHROMATOGRAPHY	Chemistry, Engineering, Agricultural Sciences	*Comprehensive two-dimensional gas chromatography: a hyphenated method with strong coupling between the two dimensions*	11	296
	COMPREHENSIVE TWO-DIMENSIONAL GAS CHROMATOGRAPHY; COMPREHENSIVE GAS CHROMATOGRAPHY COUPLED; USING COMPREHENSIVE GAS CHROMATOGRAPHIC METHODOLOGY				
13	HEAT-SENSITIVE TRP CHANNEL	Neuroscience & Behavior, Molecular Biology & Genetics, Pharmacology & Toxicology, Biology & Biochemistry	*Identification of a cold receptor reveals a general role for TRP channels in thermo sensation*	11	434
	CALCIUM-PERMEABLE TEMPERATURE-SENSITIVE CATION CHANNEL; TRP-LIKE CHANNEL EXPRESSED; TRPV4 CHANNELS (HVRL-2/MTRP12); TRP CHANNELS				

Cluster #	Name of cluster / Keywords	Top Cited Paper	Disciplines	# of Papers	Total Cites
14	ORGANIC THIN FILM TRANSISTORS	Tuning the semiconducting properties of sexithiophene by alpha, omega-substitution – alpha, omega-diperfluorohexylsexithiophene	Chemistry, Physics, Materials Science	26	415
	DITHIOPHENE-TETRATHIAFULVALENE SINGLE-CRYSTAL ORGANIC FIELD EFFECT TRANSISTORS; SOLUTION-PROCESSED ORGANIC THIN FILM TRANSISTORS; OLIGOTHIOPHENE ORGANIC THIN FILM TRANSISTORS				
15	EXOTIC THETA(+) BARYON PRODUCTION	Evidence for a narrow S = +1 baryon resonance in photoproduction from the neutron - art. no. 012002	Physics	25	1073
	THETA(+) EXOTIC BARYON; EXOTIC S = +1 BARYON; NARROW VERTICAL BAR S VERTICAL BAR=1 BARYON STATE; NARROW S = +1 BARYON RESONANCE				
16	2D STRING THEORY	Non-perturbative effects in matrix models and D-branes - art. no. 057	Physics	19	265
	TYPE 0B STRING THEORY; TWO-DIMENSIONAL STRING THEORY; C=1 MATRIX MODEL; BOUNDARY N=2 LIOUVILLE THEORY				
17	SULPHATE TRANSPORTER GENES	Pathways and regulation of sulfur metabolism revealed through molecular and genetic studies	Plant & Animal Science	17	420
	SULFATE TRANSPORTER GENES EXPRESSION; ARABIDOPSIS REVEALS GLOBAL EFFECTS; GENE EXPRESSION; ARABIDOPSIS ROOTS				
18	NARROW MESON STATE DECAYING	Observation of a narrow meson state decaying to D-s(+)pi(0) at a mass of 2.32 GeV/c(2) – art. no. 242001	Physics	16	305
	B MESON DECAYS; NARROW MESON DECAYING; NEW D-S STATE; B DECAYS				
19	TUNABLE SUPERHYDROPHOBIC SURFACES	Ultrahydrophobic surfaces. Effects of topography length scales on wettability	Materials Science, Chemistry	15	460
	TRANSPARENT SUPERHYDROPHOBIC BOEHMITE; SUPER-HYDROPHOBIC SURFACES; ALIGNED ZNO NANOROD FILMS; ULTRAHYDROPHOBIC SURFACES				
20	WILKINSON MICROWAVE PROBE	Reconstructing the primordial power spectrum	Physics, Space Science	15	223

collected together, even to the expert. An additional quarter of the time our interviewees said they had previously thought of that area as a cohesive emerging front and confirmed it was a potentially nascent emerging front. For example, two interviewees pointed to the promise of micro-fluidic analytical techniques (experiments in chemistry and biology being carried out on a small scale). In this field, ultraviolet light polymerization improves detection accuracy for lower cost (Arutyunov & Medvedeva, 1992), and two-dimensional separation systems (Gottschlich et al., 2001) and chaotic advection allow for more rapid mixing of small amounts of liquids (Liu et al., 2000). These advances may open the way for more useful chips for microscopic experiments.

The methodology is far from perfect and identified many clusters that are not, in fact, useful for identifying emerging fronts. About one quarter of the research fronts appeared to be arti-facts of a specific event or release of data, and therefore not necessarily the emerging fronts we were looking for. An example was the front surrounding NASA's Wilkinson Microwave Anisotropy Probe, which looks at differences in the Cosmic Microwave Background radiation left over from the Big Bang (Bastero-Gil, Freese, & Mersini-Houghton, 2003; Eriksen et al., 2004; Tegmark, de Oliveira-Costa, & Hamilton, 2003). Two space physicists at the University of Pennsylvania indicated that this project releases data periodically and that our identifica-tion of a high-impact cluster of papers on this topic was largely a function of the punctuated release of information, rather than some important breakthrough or area of new interest among researchers. Nevertheless, this series of experiments has provided some important new evi-dence for cosmology.

In a few other cases, it appears that we have misidentified a research front. For example, the availability of genome draft sequence and genome-analysis software, along with new large databases of human genome sequences, were used by two scientists to identify novel gene fragments and cDNAs. These articles were all by the same authors, published in the same year in a small set of journals. Our experts judged them to be the result of a specific new use of a methodological tool, rather than a new area of research. While these findings may be interesting, they do not constitute an emerging front, which is usually characterized by a broad range of authors, journals, and laboratories. For our quantitative analysis, we eliminated this front because it had an endogeneity of 62%, suggesting a misidentified or artificial front.

In most cases, interviews with experts confirmed that the emerging front procedure was indeed identifying, in large part, promising areas in science. Additionally, the methodology seemed, in most cases, to correctly select the majority of important papers and authors in the fronts during the time period.

In our case studies, we focused on four emerging clusters that our interviewees identified as among the most interesting and potentially important. We selected one front that was not multidisciplinary, two that were very multidisciplinary, and one that was somewhat multidis-ciplinary. In addition, we generated citing papers sets for each front, and analyzed bibliometric and social characteristics of these sets to better understand why the fronts emerged. In the first case study, we focused on a technical citation-based analysis of the front, and in the latter three cases on a content-based description of the field.

Our first case study is the multidisciplinary field of organic thin-film transistors, including the fields of chemistry, physics, and materials science. It is an emerging field that may lead to the manufacture of cheap and ubiquitous electronic and computing devices printed on plastic. The second case study, describing the ekpyrotic universe, was judged by physicists at different universities to be an emerging contender for explaining the creation of the universe in theoretical physics. This field was not multidisciplinary, with all its papers coming from physics.

The third front we describe deals with the amyloid precursor protein (APP), spoken of by multiple researchers as a "hot" area in Alzheimer's research because of its involvement in the pathogenesis of the disease. This research could lead to methods to block the formation of plaque, possibly the root cause of disease. This research is highly multidisciplinary, involving work in molecular biology and genetics, biology and biochemistry, and neuroscience and behavior.

The fourth front we describe is on severe acute respiratory syndrome (SARS), identified in 2004, and explores the category of coronaviruses and pandemics, which promised to be of continuing interest to the National Institutes of Health, the Centers for Disease Control and Prevention, and world health agencies. SARS research largely falls into the field of clinical medicine but has a scattering of papers in microbiology and plant and animal science, making it moderately interdisciplinary. The pandemic of 2020 has made this area of research critical—it is indeed interesting that our research method was identified before the pandemic. This research may well have contributed to the ability to find a vaccine in 2020 and distribute it in 2021.

Table 4.3 contrasts some bibliometric and social variables regarding each front. To create these statistics, we analyzed the cited and citing paper sets for each of the four fronts. Self-citation involves matching author names on cited and citing papers, and counts the number of citations where one of the citing authors on a paper matched one of the cited authors. All self-citation counts were within the expected range. The percentage of citing papers by cited authors counts the number of citing papers with one or more authors from the highly cited paper set. Hence, this measured the degree to which leading authors are still active in producing current papers, and the degree to which they were citing one another. The percentage of cited papers and citing papers in the current year measured the degree to which the research area is "front loaded", with papers in the most current year of the six-year time window used to create the cluster. For example, in the SARS and ekpyrotic universe fronts, the citing papers were all in the most recent year of the six-year frame. A high value for this measure was expected for an emerging research area based on a high volume of current papers. Finally, the endogeneity was given for each front.

Table 4.3   Case study characteristics

	APP	SARS	Thin-film transistors	Ekpyrotic universe
Self-citation rate	8.4%	9.8%	16.9%	13.6%
% citing papers by cited authors	43.3%	34.0%	39.9%	37.1%
% cited items in most recent year	61.9%	92.0%	34.6%	78.6%
% citing items in most recent year	91.7%	100%	78.9%	100%
Endogeneity	7.7%	5.0%	6.5%	13.6%

Following the discussion of each of the four cases, we present a map showing the relative positions of the highly cited papers in each front. This two-dimensional representation was generated using a force-directed placement algorithm (Small, 2006), which works by setting up attractive forces between co-cited papers and repulsive forces between all papers that vary with distance. The method attempts to arrange the papers in two dimensions such that the residual force or stress in the system is minimized.

It is interesting to note the breakdown of authorship in these papers. We coded every author of every paper in our four fronts and categorized their affiliations as academic, industry, or government, in order to get a sense of where the research was being conducted. We considered "academic" any non-profit research institution or university, "industry" any for-profit company or hospital, and "government" any government body or foundation funded largely by the government to do research. Organizations we coded as government were national and international, including Japan's Science & Technology Corporation, CERN, the World Health Organization, and various Departments of Health. The extent of industry involvement in these fronts, including companies, such as Xerox and IBM, and hospitals, such as the Mayo Clinic and Massachusetts General, as seen in Tables 4.4 and 4.5, was significant and indicative of their potential for applications as well as basic science.

Table 4.4   Affiliation of case study authors

	APP	SARS	Ekpyrotic universe	Thin-film transistors
Academic	58.44%	28.07%	83.78%	60.75%
Industry	33.77%	32.46%	0.00%	33.64%
Government	7.79%	39.47%	16.22%	5.61%

Table 4.5   Affiliations of those who cite the case studies

	APP	SARS	Ekpyrotic universe	Thin-film transistors
Academic	66.76%	48.44%	74.07%	60.86%
Industry	27.19%	26.30%	0.00%	27.53%
Government	6.05%	25.26%	25.93%	11.61%

Note: For all fronts we ran a script to code all affiliations as either "academic" or "non-academic" and found that about 64% of affiliations are academic and 36% are non-academic.

The breakdown of the author affiliations of the papers that cited the highly cited papers in our fronts had roughly similar results, with a trend toward slightly higher academic representation in all but the ekpyrotic universe front.

FOUR EMERGING FRONT CASE STUDIES

In order to understand whether the four emerging areas we studied are meaningful, we will briefly describe each of them as a case study. Quantitative research often presents results that make sense only to the computer (a problem that has become known as creating a "black box"). But we believe it is important that the areas we identified also pass a basic test for impact and coherency. As we studied each emerging front, they did indeed seem to be representing an area where scientists were building on each other's work to tackle an important problem that could result in meaningful impacts.

Organic Thin-film Transistors

Organic semiconductors, that are now used in transistors, have been known since the 1940s, and the first transistor based on an organic semiconductor was reported in 1986. The 2000 Nobel Prize in Chemistry recognized the contributions to this area by Heeger, MacDiarmid, and Shirakawa who, in the late 1970s, created semiconductors by doping the polymer poly-acetylene (Collins, 2004).

Organic thin-film transistors have attracted much interest because of their various potential uses and applications in many low-cost, large-area electronic applications, such as smart cards, radio-frequency identification tags, and flat panel displays (Sheraw et al., 2003). This offers a less costly, though slower, device than the currently available silicon technology. They are also ideal for creating compact, lightweight, mechanically flexible, and structurally interesting electronic devices because they are compatible with plastic substrates; potentially, such devices include slow but very inexpensive computers—leading to use in ubiquitous computing in anything from clothing to table-tops (Long, 1997). Conducting plastics have already been used in a number of applications, such as light-emitting diodes.

The primary performance measure of organic semiconductor quality is charge carrier mobility (μ). In the best devices based on thin organic films, values of $\mu \sim 1.5$ cm^2/V s have been reported (Podzorov et al., 2003). Other performance parameters include the on-to-off current ratio (I on/I off) and the sub-threshold swing (S) (Chesterfield et al., 2003). Various organic semiconductor systems have been studied, among which pentacene has shown the most promising performance. Pentacene has exhibited the highest field-effect mobility and is a possible candidate to complement or replace the entrenched, amorphous silicon technology in many large-area electronics applications (Afzali, Dimitrakopoulos, & Graham, 2003).

Despite progress and potential, several technical issues remain to be resolved before thin-film transistors can be in wide-scale use. Most of these issues are associated with grain boundaries and interfacial disorder in organic thin films, which are the major factors that limit the mobility, cause the dependence of the mobility on the gate voltage, and result in the broadening of the on/off transition (Podzorov et al., 2003). The contact effects in organic transistors need to be further studied, as the charge injection/extraction process at the source/drain electrodes is still poorly understood (Bürgi et al., 2003). Another important point of concern regarding organic thin-film transistors is their lifetime, both on the shelf and under operation (Gelinck et al., 2004).

This front is the largest of the new clusters in the 1999–2004 dataset. It appeared in our data in August 2004 in the form of three highly cited papers. By year-end it had grown to 26 papers, a dramatic growth that was noted by several authors (Afzali, Dimitrakopoulos, & Breen, 2002; Halik et al., 2003; Murphy et al., 2004). We found that 15 of the 228 citing papers are in the set of 26 highly cited papers, giving an endogeneity of 6.5%. The 228 citing items cited the 26 highly cited papers 460 times, and 17% of these were self-citations. The authors on the highly cited papers were also authors on 40% of the citing papers, accounting for about 50% of the citations. This means that highly cited authors were still involved in writing current papers and cited each other frequently. Thus, the leading authors were still very active in the field, reinforcing the small-world nature of this group.

Even though, technically, the cluster is a static snapshot of a six-year period, we could look at the time distribution of papers. The percentage of highly cited papers from the last year of the period (2004) was 34%, and the percentage of citing papers in the last year of the period was 79%. There is a sharp rise in number of citing papers starting in 2003 and accelerating in 2004. This coincided with the cluster's emergence in 2004. Another notable feature was the rapid expansion of the number of review papers in the citing population, which grew from three in 2003 to 24 by 2004.

The drive toward applications is very clear if we examine the cited and citing papers. All but five of the 26 highly cited papers specifically mentioned possible applications in their first paragraphs. A typical opening sentence was: "Organic field-effect transistors based on molecular and polymeric organic semiconductors are a focus of considerable current interest, motivated by their potential applications for low-cost memories, smart cards, and driving circuits for large-area display device applications" (Videlot et al., 2003). Consistent with "normal" science, the papers revealed a great deal of tweaking and tinkering with systems in order to get better electron mobility. All investigators appeared to be racing toward the same goal: finding a practical and economically viable device (Facchetti et al., 2000; Long, 1997).

Ten of the 26 papers also pointed to "significant recent progress" in their first paragraphs. This was echoed by the citing authors. One states: "Many new discoveries were brought to light during the [2003–2004] time frame" (Facchetti, Mushrush, et al., 2003; Facchetti, Yoon, et al., 2003; Mushrush et al., 2003). The progress alluded to was often the increased charge carrier mobility. Also sparking interest was the promise of cheap methods of fabrication, such as inkjet printing or the stamping of circuits directly on plastic, analogous to printing on paper.

An industrial scientist interviewed, reported that the field was currently poised between basic research and applications, what the interviewee called the "development phase," with some significant obstacles to overcome before commercialization can begin. The focus on applications and economic payoff was also reflected in the involvement of authors from companies such as Lucent, IBM, Infineon, Philips, and Xerox, often in collaboration with university partners. Overall the institutional mix of author addresses on cited papers is about 61% academic, 34% industry, and 6% government. One industry respondent also pointed to the fact that large companies are entering the field and setting up expensive multidisciplinary research teams similar to those in academia, including materials scientists, physicists, and chemists. It was suggested that these new interdisciplinary teams may in part account for the upsurge in number of publications. However, the race for commercialization has also made companies and universities more secretive about their work—for example, making collegial interactions at meetings more difficult. Often patents are applied for prior to the publication of results, which adds to the time lag for dissemination (Murray & Stern, 2005).

Thus, the emergence of this front in 2004 had to do with both an increase in activity sparked by new advances, and the increased investment of resources by academia and industry to overcome the remaining technical obstacles to commercialization. Ironically, if publication activity declines in the future, it might signal either the privatization of the field, as patenting replaces publication, or alternatively the failure of the field to overcome the remaining technical barriers (Figure 4.2).

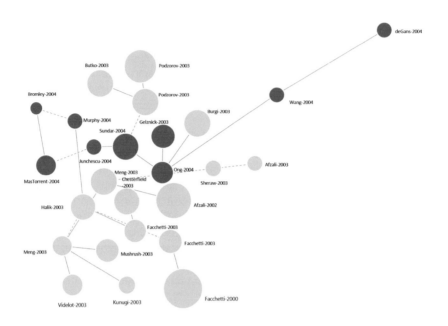

Note: Each circle on a map represents a paper whose size is proportional to its citation count. Circles of papers of the final year of the year range are one shade; circles of other papers are in a contrasting shade. The papers are connected only by the strongest normalized co-citation links for each paper (solid lines), supplemented by a small number of weak links (dashed lines) to connect the papers in a minimal spanning tree.

Figure 4.2   Organic thin-film transistors display

Ekpyrotic Universe

The word ekpyrotic is derived from the Greek word "ekpyrosis," which means con-flagration—a very large and intense fire. The ekpyrotic scenario, which is the focus of this research front, assumes a five-dimensional space-time universe, consisting of visible 3-branes and hidden 3-branes separated by a finite gap that contains an additional 3-brane, which is free to move (Khoury et al., 2001). A brane is a physical object that generalizes the notion of a point particle to higher dimensions. The model proposes that our current universe was formed through the collision of the moving brane in the extra dimension with the visible fixed brane. The universe was initially almost static, with negligible energy density; however, through the collision, the kinetic energy density was converted to radiation (Lyth, 2002). The release of hot energy led to the accelerated expansion of our universe and the start of the big bang. In the ekpyrotic model, the universe undergoes a periodic sequence of expansion and contraction, where each cycle begins with a "big bang" and ends in a "big crunch," only to emerge in a Big Bang once again. The transition from expansion to contraction is caused by introducing negative potential energy, rather than spatial curvature (Steinhardt & Turok, 2002). If the ekpyrotic universe scenario is true, it completely changes our understanding of the initial conditions in which our Big Bang occurred, and could provide answers to a number of problems that have been plaguing cosmologists for years.

For cosmologists, time began the moment the Big Bang occurred. However, the ekpyrotic universe theory suggests that the universe was contracting prior to the collision of the branes, which in turn suggests that the universe may have existed for a short time before the Big Bang took place. As a result, what we conceive to be the beginning of time may just be a bridge to a pre-existing phase of the universe (Khoury et al., 2002). Universes are created by the contraction, collision, and expansion of branes, and since they do not fully contract they become bigger after each collision. If the universe did exist for a short time before the Big Bang, this would provide alternatives to the inflationary theory and the current Big Bang model, opening a whole range of possibilities.

Our interviewees noted that the theory utilizes string theory and heterotic M-theory to provide answers to key theoretical questions of the structure of the universe. These include issues such as the flatness puzzle and the homogeneity puzzle, dealing with questions such as why the universe is so close to being spatially flat and why causally disconnected regions of the universe are so similar (Khoury et al., 2001). The ekpyrotic model assumes that our universe originated in a Bogomol'nyi–Prasad–Sommerfield state, which answers the flatness issue (Martin et al., 2002). The homogeneity puzzle is solved because the collision and initiation of the Big Bang phase occur nearly simultaneously everywhere. The questions are addressed without the use of the inflationary theory, initiating a whole new way of approaching the universe. Already admired by the cosmologists we interviewed for its scope and daring approach, if it is proved correct, the ekpyrotic universe model may help cosmologists finally unlock some secrets of the creation of our universe. As a result of the highly theoretical nature of this research, 84% of the authors in this front are affiliated with academic or purely research institutions, with the remaining 16% in government research centers, such as CERN (European Organization for Nuclear Research) (Figure 4.3).

Amyloid Precursor Protein (APP)

The front researching the amyloid precursor protein (APP) may lead scientists one step closer to understanding the pathogenesis of Alzheimer's disease. APP belongs to a group of proteins called receptors, and has several characteristics that are similar to the Notch protein. Several observations indicate that the accumulation of amyloid-β peptide (Aβ) is a common initiating event that ultimately leads to the neurodegeneration in Alzheimer's disease. However, it is unclear how Aβ induces neurodegeneration (Sisodia, 2002). Insight into APP and its cleaved fragment amyloid peptide may prove to be useful in the treatment of Alzheimer's and slow the onset of the disease, helping prevent further deterioration. The authors of the papers in this front were 58% from academia, 34% from industry and hospitals, and 8% from government health centers.

Risk factors for Alzheimer's disease include age and inheritance; however, there is evidence that APP and Aβ peptides have a central role in the early pathogenesis of the disease, regardless of primary cause (Sisodia, 2002). The abnormal cleaving of APP generates Aβ peptides that are deposited in senile plaques in the brains of aged individuals and patients with Alzheimer's disease (Leem et al., 2002), which may lead to the onset of Alzheimer's symptoms. The cleaving procedure is facilitated by proteins, such as presenilin 1 (PSEN 1) and presenilin 2 (PSEN 2), which produce amyloid peptides from APP. In fact, the majority of early-onset, autosomal-dominant familial cases of Alzheimer's disease are caused by mutations in the presenilin genes (Leissring et al., 2002).

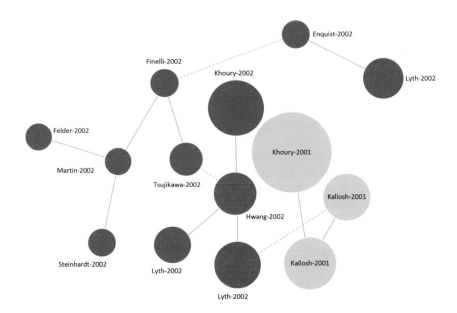

Note: Each circle on a map represents a paper whose size is proportional to its citation count. Circles of papers of the final year of the year range are one shade; circles of other papers are in a contrasting shade. The papers are connected only by the strongest normalized co-citation links for each paper (solid lines), supplemented by a small number of weak links (dashed lines) to connect the papers in a minimal spanning tree.

Figure 4.3   Ekpyrotic universe display

With the identification of the role of APP at the onset of Alzheimer's disease, scientists we interviewed believed that they may be able to develop better treatments to tackle the disease. As a result, attention is being focused on developing therapies that include the inhibition of the production of amyloid peptide (such as inhibiting the two proteolytic cleavage events that liberate amyloid peptide from APP) and the modulation of the fate and toxicity of amyloid peptide (Sisodia, 2002).

However, there are problems to overcome if this front is going to achieve breakthroughs. First, in contrast with Notch, the function of APP remains basically unknown. Second, the cytoplasmic function of APP is extremely difficult to observe, even under conditions that allow perfect detection of Aβ (Cupers et al., 2001). Nevertheless, successful research in the APP front may enable scientists to one day delay or prevent the onset of Alzheimer's disease (Figure 4.4).

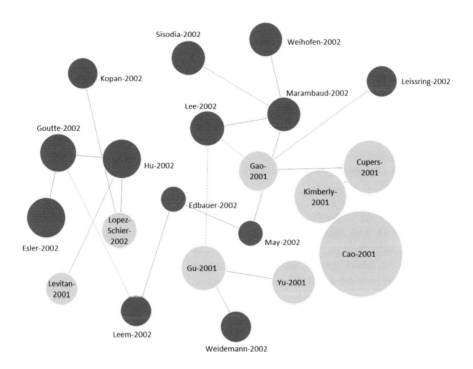

Note: Each circle on a map represents a paper whose size is proportional to its citation count. Circles of papers of the final year of the year range are one shade; circles of other papers are in a contrasting shade. The papers are connected only by the strongest normalized co-citation links for each paper (solid lines), supplemented by a small number of weak links (dashed lines) to connect the papers in a minimal spanning tree.

Figure 4.4   Amyloid precursor protein display

Severe Acute Respiratory Syndrome (SARS)

In 2004, SARS research surfaced as a prominent emerging front. This field came into enormous focus during the COVID-19 pandemic, when a vaccine was needed quickly. That this was a highly promising area of research over 15 years ago may have laid the foundations for the breakthroughs that allowed for a COVID-19 vaccine in 2020 and 2021. The final front we examined deals with research and treatment of viruses. In this case, because of the data limitations, we focused on an earlier discovered coronavirus, specifically severe acute respiratory syndrome (SARS), or SARS-CoV-1, first identified in November 2002 in the People's Republic of China. Within two months of the outbreak, SARS had become a global problem, spreading to Hong Kong, Vietnam, and Canada, and prompting the World Health Organization (WHO) to issue a global alert for the first time in more than a decade. SARS is a highly contagious disease that spreads mainly through person-to-person contact. The incubation period for SARS is usually two to seven days and is characterized by high fever followed a few days later by a dry nonproductive cough and shortness of breath (Rota et al., 2003).

   Our methodology identified SARS as an emerging front in 2003, as research attention began to turn toward it. A novel coronavirus was identified by papers in this front (Peiris et al., 2003) to be the cause of SARS. The coronaviruses are a diverse group of large, enveloped, positive-stranded RNA viruses that cause respiratory and enteric diseases in humans and animals (Rota et al., 2003). However, the SARS-associated coronavirus (SARS-CoV) is unique and does not belong to the previously known groups of coronaviruses. A characteristic of RNA viruses is the high rate of genetic mutation, which leads to the evolution of new viral strains and is a mechanism by which viruses escape host defenses. In addition, interviewees stressed that the microbiologic origins of SARS remained unclear (Tsang, 2000) and that few effective treatments were known for this infection (Hsu et al., 2003). However, at that time, the research was being conducted at an intense rate to enable early recognition of SARS and other coronaviruses, and to determine effective treatment procedures if/when the disease recurred (Ruan et al., 2003).

   Because of the importance of SARS for national safety and defense, more papers came from researchers associated with government, about 39%, than from industry/hospitals (32%) or academia (28%). This seems to be, at least partially, a feature of the health crisis in 2002, which put government emergency teams, such as the British Columbia Center for Disease Control, the "Virus Units" of various governments, and researchers at WHO, in a position to learn valuable information about the disease (Figure 4.5).

Note: Each circle on a map represents a paper whose size is proportional to its citation count. Circles of papers of the final year of the year range are one shade; circles of other papers are in a contrasting shade. The papers are connected only by the strongest normalized co-citation links for each paper (solid lines), supplemented by a small number of weak links (dashed lines) to connect the papers in a minimal spanning tree.

Figure 4.5   *SARS display*

Studying concrete examples of emerging fronts has allowed us to judge whether our methodology squares with our qualitative intuition. Studying these four areas gives us confidence that we are identifying coherent and meaningful areas of potentially promising research. We found the clear importance of SARS research in 2003 to be interesting because it may well have enabled the progress in the field that allowed for breakthrough COVID-19 vaccines. Both expert interviews as well as case studies confirm that emerging fronts identified through a clustering approach are meaningful and promising in the real world.

QUANTITATIVE ANALYSIS

We now turn from qualitative analysis to quantitative analysis. It is important, as we argue for the importance of identifying and studying emerging fronts, that the clusters we identified are both meaningful and useful. Thus, once we identified clusters we categorized them to identify patterns and test their importance. We measured, for example, whether the fronts were growing or shrinking, the extent to which they were self-referential or multidisciplinary, and to what extent they were still part of basic science or applied. Such characteristics help to establish whether the clustering methodology is intuitively meaningful, but they can also be used as independent variables to see if some cluster characteristics can be correlated to more future success. Even if these distinctions are crude, we should be able to see if they are meaningful. If so, this would suggest more research (and more granular categorizations) would be valuable avenues for future research.

Variables

Growing, Shrinking, Stable, Emerging, and Exiting Fronts: To explore the trends in nascent research, we constructed some variables to assist in our analysis. Following previous work on emerging fronts (Morris & Moore, 2000; Small, 2003), we measured the growth rates of fronts from the 1998–2003 dataset to the 1999–2004 dataset, and categorized them as growing, stable, or shrinking. *Growing fronts* are those that had more papers in our 1999–2004 period than the sum of all of their contributing fronts in the 1998–2003 analysis. A "contributing front" means that at least one paper from an earlier front is in a later front. Similarly, *shrinking fronts* are those that were smaller than the sum of all their contributing fronts in the previous time period, and *stable fronts* are those for which the sum of all contributing fronts yielded the same number of papers. *Emerging fronts* are fronts in the 1999–2004 dataset that contained no papers from the 1998–2003 dataset. *Exiting fronts* were fronts that existed in the 1998–2003 analysis but had no papers in any front in the 1999–2004 analysis. Some basic statistics about fronts are given in Table 4.6.

   Endogeneity: As noted above, the extent to which the cited papers set overlaps with the citing papers set for the front, may be an important aspect of its potential growth, provided that the overlap is not the result of an artifact, such as a single journal issue. A front that has a high cited/citing overlap is said to have high endogeneity and reflects the compression of cited and citing generations. Scientists in such a front may have a better chance of building on each other's work quickly and creating a "cohesive paradigm" (Pfeffer, 1993).

Table 4.6   *Summary statistics by front type*

Front Stats	Emerging	Growing	Stable	Shrinking	Exiting*
# of Fronts	1,837	622	1,374	1,405	1,931
% of Fronts	35.07%	18.29%	40.40%	41.31%	36.65%
# of M-D Fronts	508	268	282	396	417
% of M-D Fronts	27.65%	43.09%	20.52%	28.19%	21.60%
Average Size	2.65	8.35	2.75	4.98	2.44
Average Year	2002.57	2001.60	2000.67	2000.72	2000.24
Average Citations	83.83	557.97	283.84	510.62	189.05
Average # of Disciplines	1.30	1.61	1.22	1.36	1.23
Endogeneity	2.14	2.69	0.90	1.40	–

Notes: * Exiting front numbers were calculated based on the prior dataset (1998–2003) since, by definition, they were not present in our "up to date" dataset (1999–2004). M-D = multidisciplinary. – Not available in our data range.

As seen in the last row of Table 4.6, the level of endogeneity was generally higher among emerging fronts than among existing fronts. Additionally, growing fronts clearly displayed larger than average levels of endogeneity.

Multidisciplinarity: We constructed a variable for cluster multidisciplinarity by creating a Herfindahl index of the distribution of disciplines of the papers comprising the front. We did this by summing the squared percentage distribution of each front in each discipline. This marks the extent to which a front was composed of one main discipline or split between many disciplines. The closer a front is to having a multidisciplinary concentration score of 1.0, the closer it is to being composed of one discipline only, and the closer it is to zero, the more it is fragmented between many disciplines.

Percentage Non-academic: For all authors, we coded whether their affiliation was "academic" or "non-academic"—i.e., academic vs. government or industry. We found that academic institutions almost always had "univ," "school," "coll," "insti," or "ecol" in their titles. Some academic institutions were exceptions, so we added a number of more institution-specific filters, such as "Berkeley," "MIT," "Harvard," "polytechnic," "politec-nico," and "polytechnique," among others. We did not differentiate between government and industry in this variable because we found no generalizable way to do so for the thousands of institutions represented (with the exception of hospitals, which usually have "hosp" in their titles). We found that the percentage of academic (64%) and non-academic (36%) affiliations matched those in our four case studies, which we coded manually.

Models

For regressions, we choose to contrast two dependent variables that comprised the fates of successful research fronts—emergence and absorption. The first dependent variable, used to measure emergence, was a percentage increase of the front's growth (in number of papers) from the first period to the second. Since a growing front implies that more papers were drawn into its existing paradigm, this measure is meant to reflect the extent to which the front is emerging as a distinct area of research. The second dependent variable, measuring absorption, counts the percentage change in number of citations received by the papers in a front. This is meant to reflect the extent to which the front's knowledge is being "absorbed" or incorporated into other research. The extent to which these dependent variables differ determined whether a front focuses on "absorption" of its findings or "emergence" as a distinct area.

Our independent variables of interest were a continuous variable for multidisciplinarity, the Herfindahl index of discipline concentration, and a variable for endogeneity, which measures the percentage of citing papers that were also cited papers. For both regressions we controlled for the size of the cluster, the number of citations a cluster has received and the average year of publication for papers within the cluster, the percentage of authors in a cluster who are affiliated with non-academic institutions, and the discipline code(s) of the cluster.

Additionally, in each regression we controlled for the other dependent variable to further show the divergence of the two trends for fronts—i.e., for the regression predicting percentage change in papers, we controlled for percentage change in citations, and for the regression predicting percentage change in citations, we controlled for percentage change in papers. We included these last two controls to counter the natural collinearity of citations and number of papers. In other words, we expected size and number of citations to grow in tandem; however, we were interested in quantifying the incremental variation of citations after accounting for the increasing (decreasing) size of a front, as well as the incremental variation of growth after accounting for increasing (decreasing) citations. All regressions were reported using robust (Huber–White) standard errors.

RESULTS

The differences in direction between our two response variables of emergence and absorption were stronger than expected. Among these "hot" research fronts we found that somewhat different mechanisms led to fronts that maximize emergence, measured by how fast a front is growing, and absorption, measured by increase in citations.

In our front absorption model, using increase in total citations as the dependent variable, we found that the coefficient for multidisciplinarity was not significant, while endogeneity was negative and significant. In the front emergence model, using front growth as the dependent variable, we regressed cluster growth on the same independent variables. The coefficients for both endogeneity and multidisciplinarity were positive and statistically significant.

The size and direction of the coefficients of our control variables were as expected. In the front emergence model, the control variable for number of papers was positive and significant, indicating that larger fronts tended to grow faster. Conversely, though again as expected, in the front absorption model we found that the coefficient for number of papers was negative and significant, indicating that smaller fronts tended to grow citations faster, as a percentage increase. Average age of papers was positive for citations but negative for growth, perhaps because older fronts remained distinct and were not absorbed, indicating a survival bias over time. Percentage of author affiliations from non-academic institutions was not significant in either model. This may be due to the confounding of government and industry involvement in non-academic affiliations, but our best attempts to further divide these two classes of affiliation and add them to the model did not yield more significant results. In both models the controls for discipline, accomplished via 21 dummy variables, were statistically significant as a group. To establish the significance of these, we jointly tested the 21 discipline dummy variables using a Wald test. After some exploratory analysis we found that emerging fronts, controlling for size, tended to be more multidisciplinary, on average, than fronts in general, perhaps implying a general trend toward increasing multidisciplinarity in recent years. For a validity check we exchanged our key independent variables with the dependent variables in our models and re-ran the regressions. These models indicated identical trends to the original models in both direction and significance.

One of our more interesting findings was the sign change for endogeneity between our two models. As seen in the correlation table (Table 4.7; see also Table 4.8), the correlation between endogeneity and both of our response variables was positive and significant prior to controlling for any cluster characteristics. We explored the change of direction in more detail by building up our front absorption model step-by-step to fully understand how the predictors interrelate to explain the growth of research fronts. The sign change occurred as soon as we controlled for the percentage growth in number of papers, and it persisted through the addition of all other explanatory variables.

Table 4.7   Coefficients of regression analysis and descriptive statistics, linear regressions

	(1)	(2)
Dependent Variable:	*Emergence*	*Absorption*
	% growth papers	*% growth citations*
Independent Variables		
Multidisciplinary	0.121*	(0.077)
Endogeneity	0.038***	(0.096)***
# of Papers (size)	0.033***	(0.033)**
Avg Age of Papers	(0.035)*	0.320***
% Growth Papers		1.714***
% Growth Citations	0.208***	
% Industry Affiliations	(0.015)	0.027
Total Citations	(0.001)***	0.001
Discipline Code (dummy vars)	*sig ***	*sig *** *
Constant	70.525*	(640.478)**
N	3,401	3,401
r^2	0.448	0.427
RMSE	0.451	1.294
F	9.679***	26.800***

Notes: *** $p <0.001$; ** $p <0.01$; *$p <0.05$; *sig.* = significant. Discipline Code dummy variables were tested for joint significance using a Wald test.

The simple characteristics of clusters identified were meaningful in predicting emerging front success. The key we were looking for was whether the emerging fronts we identified grew or shrank. The results above are largely supportive of our core belief that cluster characteristics do matter for cluster success along intuitive lines (suggesting that we are identifying something real).

Table 4.8   *Descriptive statistics, correlations*

		1	2	3	4	5	6	7	8	9
1	Multidisciplinary	–								
2	# of Papers (size)	0.140*	–							
3	Total Citations	0.127*	0.699*	–						
4	New Front	0.026	-.2221*	-0.308*	–					
5	% Growth Papers	0.098*	0.243*	0.018		–				
6	% Growth Citations	0.055*	0.079*	-0.041		0.614	–			
7	Endogeneity	0.007	0.266*	-0.055*	0.131*	0.258*	0.114*	–		
8	Avg Age of Papers	0.057*	0.026	-0.249*	0.538*	0.233*	0.300*	0.340*	–	
9	% Industry Affiliations	0.015	0.007	0.052*	0.001	-0.005	0.005	-0.033	0.020	–
	Obs	6,985	6,985	6,985	6,985	4,592	4,592	6,985	6,985	6,985
	Mean	0.21	4.63	373.47	0.34	0.99	1.55	1.73	2001.49	0.36
	S.D.	0.24	5.32	661.22	0.47	0.70	1.94	2.55	1.51	0.27
	Min	–	2.00	6.00	–	0.05	0.02	–	1999	0
	Max	752,551	50.00	8,417	1.00	8.33	62.18	19.60	2004	1

Note: * Denotes significance at the $\alpha = .05$ level using the Bonferroni correction for multiple pairwise tests.

CONCLUSION

We have shown how we might be able to identify emerging research fronts and argue that it is important to do so. Research fronts provide a way to study areas of science that scientists find useful, and also reveal important insights into how new scientific knowledge is incorporated into existing research (Birnbaum, 1981b; Kuhn, 1962; Small, 1999, 2003). Qualitatively, we interviewed researchers in industry and academia to establish the reliability and effectiveness of our method for identifying "hot" areas of emerging research. Quantitatively, we focused on differentiating between fronts that maximize their "absorption" or impact by being highly cited by others (at the cost of being less distinct as their knowledge is incorporated into broader research) and fronts that maximize their "emergence" or size by growing more as a distinct, cohesive unit. We show that there are fundamental differences in the structure of these two sorts of successful research fronts. This may affect the way science as a whole absorbs or splinters-off into new areas of research, and may have important consequences for its evolution and development over time.

We found multidisciplinary research fronts to be disproportionately represented among emerging fronts, with bigger fronts tending to be more multidisciplinary and positively associated with cluster emergence and growth. Perhaps this implies that fronts that span traditional research fields are harder for a single area to absorb and digest, and therefore tend to remain more distinct. Examining the dynamic consequences of this possibility would be fruitful for future research.

We also studied how the cohesiveness or "endogeneity" of a cluster—the percentage of a cluster's citing papers that were also cited papers—affects cluster growth and impact. While endogeneity was positively associated with research fronts that are growing, it is negatively associated with research fronts in which knowledge is being absorbed via increased citation. Further, endogeneity was highest among new and growing clusters. This lends support to Kuhn's speculations, and the work of Crane and Pfeffer, on the importance of intellectual cohesiveness or paradigm strength in creating a distinct research perspective. This is potentially because high endogeneity can be seen as a crude sign of a more comprehensive, explanatory intellectual framework (Crane, 1972; Kuhn, 1962; Pfeffer, 1993).

These observations, overall, provide insight into how science changes. In our two models, the characteristics of research fronts that are associated with front growth are very different from the characteristics that are associated with front impact. Research fronts that grow are associated with multidisciplinarity and tend to be more endogenous. Research fronts that receive increased citations, on the other hand, tend not to be endogenous, and the coefficient for multidisciplinarity is not significant when controlling for other factors.

Research that has a high impact is more likely to become accepted wisdom and "change" or "evolve" the field from within in an incremental way (Collins, 1997; McCain, 1987). On the other hand, research that grows as a distinct front is more likely to lead to fragmentation— evolving into a distinct subfield or even becoming a new field entirely (Fleming, 2001; Fleming & Sorenson, 2001). Further historical analyses examining the antecedents of paradigm shifts—periods of paradigm disruption and change—would help test this conjecture.

To provide support for our method of identifying research fronts, we interviewed experts in the field—scientists who worked in an area or a closely related area—and asked them to judge how successfully the algorithm identified the research area. We found strong expert support that we identified real new fronts with high potential and that, where relevant, we identified them early in their development.

As the methods for identifying and analyzing "hot" and emerging research fronts improve, we believe this methodology will be increasingly useful to those in industry R&D, venture capitalists, government policymakers and grant givers, and individual researchers wishing to gain insight into the areas of science that are the most interesting and have the most promise.

5. Conclusion

In this book, we propose an additional organizing principle for innovation in science and technology: powerful, hidden "knowledge communities" for collaboration. In Chapter 2, we looked at knowledge communities in order to try to understand why they experience differential success. In so doing, we examined how knowledge communities build on prior knowledge and use rhetoric, in terms of flexibility, uniqueness, and cohesiveness. Knowledge communities, we argued, are a kind of mysterious interorganizational form that can have sustained and meaningful characteristics over time. In Chapter 3, we examined knowledge communities from the bottom up—we saw how and why individual researchers join and collaborate within these communities. We found that these communities can confer significant advantages to researchers and studied how researchers' position between and within these communities can influence the impact of their work. We also checked the conclusions we came to in Chapters 2 and 3, by applying our methods and hypotheses in each to the other's dataset, generalizing our findings statistically. In Chapter 4, we explored potential antecedents to knowledge communities—research fronts. By looking at the highly cited "hot" areas of science and seeing whether they maximize growth in size or citations, we were able to suggest some potential insights into how science evolves and changes, both in structure and content.

As discussed, most research on innovation and performance either takes formal organizations, like firms or universities, as the primary unit of analysis, or contrasts firms with traditional communities (Chen et al., 2002; Gittelman, 2003; Hargens, 2000b; Podolny & Stuart, 1995). In our study of innovation and performance, we took informal interorganizational knowledge communities as our unit of analysis, contrasting these communities to firms to understand how innovation and performance happens and how it can be best promoted. Technologists envision a new blockchain-based version of the Internet using cryptocurrency where digital interaction and exchange can be created, owned and run directly by communities.

The examination of the performance implications of innovative knowledge communities focused on the informal connections between researchers and on how these connections drive performance. Besides firms, universities, NGOs, and research centers, there exists unappreciated interorganizational knowledge communities of researchers who share similar research subjects and goals and who build on each other's ideas. These communities can be intense and distinct, with their own norms of research and methodology, and internal languages—richly textured and interesting units for analysis.

Chapters 2 and 3, taken together, provide a picture of how such communities work in relation to individual performance on the micro and macro levels. Chapter 4 provides some indication of what promotes the forming or splintering of these communities. Chapter 2, "Innovating knowledge communities: an analysis of group collaboration and competition in science and technology," explored the macro incentives that affect the performance of knowledge communities. We looked at two dimensions of these communities: the use of rhetoric and the use of knowledge. For each of these dimensions, we explored how flexible, cohesive, and unique they are compared to other knowledge communities. In seeking to understand the differential performance of knowledge communities over time, we developed six hypotheses in this chapter, three about knowledge and three about rhetoric. The first argues that innovating communities that draw from diverse sources of knowledge will perform better; the second that innovating communities that are flexible in their use of knowledge will perform better; the third that innovative communities that are unique in their use of knowledge will perform better. Then the fourth hypothesis holds that innovating communities that use similar rhetoric will perform better; the fifth that innovating communities that use stable rhetoric will perform better; and lastly, the sixth, that innovating communities that use mainstream rhetoric will perform better.

While all of our hypotheses were confirmed, we found that these two dimensions, rhetoric and knowledge, push clusters in different directions. Knowledge communities do best if they are flexible, dispersed, and unique in their use of knowledge, as measured by patterns of backward citations. On the other hand, knowledge communities do best if they are stable, cohesive, and generic in their use of rhetoric. We conclude that the use of rhetoric and knowledge, as well as the management of the tension between them, is an important driver of success for a knowledge community. This chapter modelled some of the community-wide characteristics that can help predict and explain the performance of knowledge communities over time.

Chapter 3, "Positioning knowledge: knowledge communities and new knowledge creation," explored the micro identifications and incentives that correlate with and affect the performance of knowledge creators with respect to knowledge communities. We presented three hypotheses in this chapter. The first argued that new knowledge has more impact if it is within a knowledge community than if it is not. The second hypothesis argued that a position toward the intellectual semi-periphery of a knowledge community results in greater new knowledge impact than a position at the center or periphery of a knowledge community. Lastly, two competing third hypotheses argued that creators of new knowledge who have greater impact, actively engage in either multiple or in very few knowledge communities.

We used positioning theory and search theory to help explain our findings, firstly, that knowledge positioned within a knowledge community tended to have greater impact than knowledge positioned outside. Secondly, that within a knowledge community, knowledge positioned at the semi-periphery tends to have more impact than knowledge at the core or the very periphery. These positionings were established by discerning how different the citation structure of any given paper is from the "average" citation structure of other papers in that cluster, as operationalized by the dot product of the vector between the centroid of the cluster and any specific paper. Also, we showed that the value of experience with many knowledge communities is moderated by the impact of the author. This chapter examined how knowledge communities influence and reflect incentives on a paper-by-paper level of analysis, explaining from a bottom-up perspective how knowledge communities function.

In the comparative analysis that concluded this chapter, our computer science data were analyzed via this chapter's methods on a paper-by-paper basis. We found that papers with solely firm-affiliated authors and papers with mixed firm- and academic-affiliated authors had, on average, greater impact than papers from authors solely affiliated with academic institutions.

Chapter 4, "Emerging research fronts in science and technology: identifying breakout ideas early," explored the early formation of successful or effective knowledge communities.

We identified the very small cohesive groups, which we call "fronts," that receive the most citations throughout the disciplines of hard science and examined how the knowledge they produce is incorporated into their field. We explored two ways knowledge could be incorporated: by attracting more papers into its cluster (what we call knowledge "growth") or by maximizing the citations it received by other papers (knowledge "absorption"). We speculated that knowledge growth contributes most to the formation of new knowledge communities or that fragmenting knowledge communities create new niches and areas of study. Knowledge absorption probably best helps explain the change of knowledge communities over time. This chapter was more exploratory than a test of established propositions. We developed a new methodology for identifying research fronts and used interviews to test the validity of our assumptions.

WHAT AUTHOR AFFILIATION MEANS FOR IMPACT

We focused on understanding what characteristics drive differential success of knowledge communities, why and how these knowledge communities create incentives for their members, and how the knowledge from young emerging knowledge "fronts" is either absorbed by its field or grows as an independent area of research. One of the most interesting things about knowledge communities is the diversity of organizations that play a role in them—universities, firms, governments, standards agencies, think tanks, trade associations, international NGOs, hospitals, and so on.

For the computer science dataset, we were able to more clearly delineate between firms and academic institutions. As we discussed in Chapter 2, research in academia is increasingly becoming commercialized (Henderson et al., 1998; Jaffe & Lerner, 2001; Shane, 2002). This is particularly true in computer science; examples such as Google come to mind.

We also coded the affiliations of the authors for the computer science database. Data exploration found virtually no authors in this field with government affiliations, so we coded each organization as either academic or industry. In this case our results provided significant results. We coded papers with only firm authors as "pure firm," only academic authors as "pure academic," and any mix of academic and firm authors as "firm/academic mix." For each paper and each cluster, we also coded the percentage of authors who were academic (counting multiple authors from the same institution multiple times in each case). From this we hope to begin to understand how firms and their members participate in knowledge communities.

For this coding of affiliations in our original results in Chapter 2, we found that, overall, knowledge communities with higher proportions of papers with only industry affiliations, as compared to papers with authors solely affiliated with academic institutions, generally perform better. Increasing the proportion of papers from authors with mixed industry and academic affiliations is generally not significant, but is sometimes associated with decreased knowledge community performance when both are contrasted to purely academically affiliated papers.

In Chapter 4, we discussed four research fronts in detail. For these four case studies, we coded all author affiliations for our fronts manually, and coded both the papers in these fronts and the papers citing these fronts as government, academic, and industry. We found that about 10% of the organizations involved with these four fronts—organic thin-film transistors, ekpyrotic universe, amyloid precursor protein, and severe acute respiratory syndrome—were governments or NGOs, about 30% were industry (firms, hospitals), and about 60% were primarily from an academic institution. Reviewing this work, we found patterns we could use to generalize author affiliations for the complete database. Academic institutions, for example, almost always had "univ," "school," "coll," "insti," or "ecol" in their titles. We looked through the most frequently recurring words, and found some academic institutions that were exceptions, some further keywords, such as "Harvard," "MIT," and "Caltech," and some keywords specific to foreign university systems, such as "polytechnic," "politecnico," and "polytechnique." Government-affiliated groups and firms were largely idiosyncratic.

Because of the complexity of the data, we decided to simply bifurcate affiliations as academic and non-academic, to get the most reliable results. When a paper had multiple authors from the same institutions, we counted the institutions each time (e.g., a paper with three authors from Yale and one from Pfizer was coded as 75% academic). This does not delineate between government organizations and firms, but it is a reasonable compromise considering that there were over 50,000 unique organizations in the database (over 25,000 papers in the 1998–2004 database, and multiple authors per paper). We found, consistent with the four case studies we coded manually, that 61% of the organizations in emerging fronts were academic and 39% were non-academic organizations. We added the percentage of fronts that were non-academic into our regression and found that it was not a significant predictor in any of our analyses. Furthermore, there were no changes of direction or significance among our other predictors (see Table 2.1 from our original analysis).

LIMITATIONS

Several limitations could undermine the strength of our findings. Some are a result of a scarcity of work on performance-oriented research using these methodologies. This makes us more cautious in interpreting the results and relying on new methodologies without the support of extant research. Further research would address many of these qualifications.

Our methodology of clustering finds clusters of papers with similar citation structures, but interpreting these clusters is somewhat new to management research. A long history of research in the sociology of science and the sociology of knowledge suggests these do indeed mark intellectually similar groups of researchers working on similar problems (Gmur, 2003; Small, 2003). However, this methodology is based on citation patterns that, as an imperfect heuristic, raise some concerns. A citation represents recognition by a researcher that an idea is relevant to or contributed to his or her research. As such, the citation indicates agreement or disagreement. Further, there could be alternative explanations for why a citation is made—such as citation of "token" papers that represent a topic but are not truly influential to an author, citations to a mentor or a senior scholar (citations of respect), or citations because of personal ties to others one has met or interacted with.

Indeed, as shown in Chapter 2, the average number of citations per paper grew quickly over the past few decades, as citation programs, such as EndNote and others, as well as computerized resources, have made citing easier. At the same time, these resources have made knowledge flow quicker and more accessible to more people. The qualifications to the meaning of citations are not such a problem, we believe, for the clustering methodology of this chapter. We cluster in order to try to identify cohesive intellectual groups; citation patterns that, rather than representing knowledge contributions, are norm- or relationship-based may indeed be a useful way of identifying a group with shared norms and high interaction.

These concerns are more troublesome for our dependent variables—citation counts and cumulative counts of papers. We counted citation levels for a paper as "impact" and accumulated numbers of papers as some measure of community "success"—there are clearly heuristics for underlying variables of contribution and importance, respectively. However, as discussed, a paper may receive citations or be published for many reasons. In Chapter 2, we assumed that more papers meant community success (with a robustness check using aggregate citations), and in Chapter 3, we contrasted paper numbers and citation counts as alternate dependent variables. In Chapter 4, we assumed that high citation rates meant higher impact. But higher citation counts can, as we have discussed, mean many things, from reputation, to prestige of school, to network of friends, to, of course, knowledge impact. A paper might be published for many reasons—as a test of another theory, as a new theory, or as a comment on or literature review of the theories of others.

A related field dealing with similar issues is that of patents. As with this analysis, patent citations are often used to mark impact. Trajtenberg (1990) argued that patent counts do correlate highly with the commercial value of patents and their profitability. Similarly, other studies have used the existence of patents and their patent classes as heuristics for the intellectual capital in a company or that company's research history. Many of the objections we raised are appropriate in this context as well, but scholars generally recognize the qualifications and assume that patents, and patent counts, are meaningful and, where possible, control for those aspects of patents that would detract from this assumption. Here, we tried to control for paper characteristics that would artificially obfuscate the relationship between the dependent and the main independent variables, such as school and journal prestige, year, and bibliography size (or average bibliography size), among other characteristics. Overall, we believe that with appropriate controls, citation count is an appropriate heuristic for impact, and paper count is a proxy for importance. At the same time, we recognize the limitations this assumption places on our findings.

A second potential problem is our implicit assumption that a paper that is published or presented at a conference represents "knowledge creation" or "new knowledge." We have tried not to imply that all new papers represent "innovations," though it is clear, particularly in scientific fields, that at least some do. We used papers as our units of analysis—rather than authors, schools, journals, or "ideas"—partly because we assume that each paper represents a discrete piece of work with a coherent idea or contribution. The institutional mechanisms of journals and conferences, and the incentive structure of academia (emphasizing paper publications), makes this assumption less troubling.

On another note, we argue that knowledge communities are important markers of intellectual boundaries—that our authors' position between and among them matters for their impact, and that their shape and structure is important for aggregate impact (Fleming, 2001). But this raises an endogeneity problem—if some positions or some schools were advantageous, then why wouldn't authors position themselves there, gaining this advantage in the short term though reducing it in the medium term (Abrahamson, 1996; Abrahamson & Piazza, 2019; Aksom, 2021)? This question is analogous to the well-known arguments in economics about market entrance when profits are abnormally high. While this conscious maneuvering by researchers does exist, a few factors mitigate its ability to arbitrage away the sustained differences between these communities.

Knowledge communities are real communities with shared norms, characteristics, and networks for relationships. Simply adjusting a paper's bibliography structure may fool the algorithm used in these papers into thinking a paper belongs to a certain knowledge community, but it is unlikely to fool the initiated in that community, or to result in any advantages to that paper. As we discussed in Chapter 3, various real costs of time, learning, and networking are required to enter into a knowledge community, even at the periphery—all incurred before one can either reap the advantages of being in a knowledge community or be a part of it. Further, knowledge of the delineations of knowledge communities is variable and somewhat blurry. Unlike with formal organizations, there are no clear lines of in/out but rather more amorphous delineations. One might enter a knowledge community because of training, or a mentor, or interest. Even most scientists or engineers cannot, for example, become researchers in thin-film transistors overnight because it has become a "hot" field.

From our interviews, we believe that researchers have a relatively keen interest in and a mental representation of, the knowledge structure of their field—but not necessarily a completely accurate one. This leads to uncertainty about where to position research and a lack of consensus about where it would be advantageous to do so. Therefore, the constant evolution and dynamic changes of knowledge communities seen in Chapter 2 suggest that knowledge communities are not static—further compounding the complexity of conscious positioning because the efficacy of a position must be predicted in the future. Lastly, while authors are attracted to areas where their knowledge will have impact, or where "interesting" research is being done, this does not mean that researchers' end, or only end, is to maximize this positioning. Researchers are often genuinely interested in their ideas, are intellectually and psychologically committed to their current area of research, and have significant path dependencies, particularly in terms of accumulated knowledge and relationships, which will often be more valuable in maximizing citations than position. Indeed, position only accounts for some of the variance in citation count. Other factors, such as quality of the idea, quality of the research, knowledge and relationships of the author, and luck, account for the majority of the variance in impact and importance of a paper. Therefore, to a large extent the position of a paper is a result and expression of these factors rather than strategy, although the correlation holds.

SYNTHESIS BETWEEN CHAPTERS

We converge on several conclusions. It is clear how important it is for researchers to help improve their rate of innovation and impact. Indeed, knowledge positioning made a significant difference on research impact and direction. Research, sometimes thought of as an individualistic process or one guided by general trends in technology, turns out to be also a deeply social process. Indeed, sociologists of science, such as Latour and Fuchs, would be gratified to find that knowledge communities make such a difference in performance, because this lends some quantitative support to their arguments that knowledge is, at least partly, socially constructed at the community level.

In all cases, some measure of endogeneity mattered. Though endogeneity was measured in different time frames in the three main chapters, we define it as the extent to which a knowledge community uses knowledge from its own group—i.e., cites other papers in that grouping (Pfeffer, 1993). This measure was positive and significant in measuring the impact of a paper and the growth of knowledge communities and research fronts. Endogeneity was negative, controlling for percentage growth of a front, in measuring the impact a paper had (though impact was positive and significant without controlling for the percentage growth of a front). The importance of endogeneity in all these contexts lends support, we believe, to the idea that knowledge that builds on a tight community of other knowledge will, in aggregate, perform better.

We believe endogeneity can be seen as a heuristic for how cohesive, meaningful, and comprehensive the intellectual framework is that a group provides to its members in a specific context—not an extensive framework for viewing the world, but a framework for solving a particular related set of problems (Lodahl & Gordon, 1972). A group is a social construction to provide shared meaning, coordinate research, facilitate intergroup communication, and create a reciprocal and collaborative community, and is a vital way for an individual researcher to filter information and direct interconnected research—which also highlights the interconnected nature of technology and science (Lodahl & Gordon, 1972; Pfeffer, 1993). We stated in many places that knowledge communities, though they are informal organizations without formal structure, can be seen as having leadership, core capacities, durable characteristics, and differentiated success.

In formal organizations, this shared social construction is often attributed to the CEO's leadership and vision. Endogeneity—repeated interactions and shared learning—is the visible mechanism through which the spirit of the knowledge community is shared. Other unobserved ways include conferences and verbal and written communication outside of academic publications. That so many characteristics often attributed to the structure and leadership of a firm exist in groups without formal leaders or formal structure, suggests value in reexamining formal organizations with this in mind; it is a perspective supportive of central elements in the resource-based view (Pfeffer, 1993).

EXTENSIONS

Future work on knowledge communities can build on our findings, which combine work in the sociology of knowledge on paradigms and clusters with the strategic literature on performance. How do large network structures and clustered small-world social structure affect the performance of firms and individuals in a broader context? How do differing contexts affect the existence, impact, and nature of knowledge communities? Two aspects of our work might be valuably extended. First, our methodology could be applied to diverse settings as a new "metric" for analysis. Second, our core ideas could be extended and tested in different contexts.

Our methodology extends and builds on the research from the sociology of knowledge, which studies clusters of knowledge, and uses additional methods from computer science and genomic sequencing to allow for the identification of cohesive knowledge clusters of similar work, while allowing most work to remain outside of a cluster, using links between nodes. This method has the potential to allow for the identification of in/out groups, cohesive intellectual communities, and other groupings of similar nodes in a variety of contexts. Importantly, this method does not require ex ante for each member to choose to be a member of one group or another—groups form because of their content, not because of conscious labels. Such clustering could be done on patent citations, paper citations, patterns of words in a written document, patterns of formulas in an Excel spreadsheet, Internet links and web pages, and so on. Researchers of the "small world" phenomenon have found large-scale ways of measuring whether a context has small world properties; this method allows for the more specific identification of cluster location and the subsequent analysis of cluster characteristics (Uzzi & Spiro, 2005)—potentially useful to researchers in many contexts.

Our current analysis examined the existence of knowledge communities in a variety of contexts: social science (management), hard science (selected papers across a broad spectrum), and technical science (computer science). While we focused on performance—at individual, group, and organizational levels of analysis—we do so in a setting that is largely academic, though often deeply intertwined with firms and government, among other organizations. If we were to take patents as our unit of analysis, for example, and cluster them, we would likely find clusters corresponding to tightly interconnected knowledge. But the qualities of such clusters might be significantly different in different contexts. We have argued that clusters in a context of knowledge creation represent communities of researchers with similar interests working on similar problems. In a patent context, the nature of collaboration might be significantly different to match the different motives and incentives in an industry setting. In this setting, knowledge has proprietary value, since research is most valuable if it is private. Citations are made less to recognize contributions than to place a patent in a specific context and to establish its legitimacy and territory. Valuable knowledge may go unpatented in order to keep others from using it, or patents may be filed merely to "block" other firms. While these do not represent major impediments to a rather robust methodology, particularly since these deviations from the standard meaning of a citation are systematic, they will require additional conceptualization of the meaning and interpretation of clusters (Murray, 2005; Murray & Stern, 2005).

Another path for extending the current analysis within the context of knowledge communities in an innovation context is to turn our data around and, rather than examining how papers position themselves among knowledge communities, examine how firms associated with papers position themselves in knowledge communities (Rosenkopf & Nerkar, 2001). For example, it may be that firms that deeply connect with growing and vibrant knowledge communities are able to commercialize on this growth. The rise of Google, for example, whose founders wrote one of the top articles in the knowledge community on "Internet search," corresponds with the rise of this community. Alternatively, other companies might be well served bridging more established knowledge communities—drawing on the ideas of different communities and synthesizing them to create commercializable products or ideas (Henderson et al., 1998). This could be done directly by looking at the affiliations of authors and, for those authors affiliated with specific firms, seeing how this affects their patenting performance, market performance or "intellectual impact" in their field (Shane, 2002). There also exists a link whereby patents cite papers and papers cite patents. In a context where academic research and patenting are strongly linked, such as biotechnology, we believe this might be a fascinating way to cluster the academic literature and then see how this clustering affects corresponding value in the patent context—essentially studying how ideas get commercialized (Ali & Gittelman, 2015; Gittelman & Kogut, 2003; Jayaraj & Gittelman, 2017). Central to such analysis would be the identification of knowledge communities within the academic setting, and perhaps the patent setting.

The combination of a relatively underexplored unit of analysis—clusters—and a deep history of research on how communities function and interact, now operationalized and testable, allows for many other potential extensions. Such extensions may allow the study of differential success in communities and help explain individual and group performance through an examination of large network structures.

POLICY IMPLICATIONS

This research provides insight into how science, social science, and technology build on previous findings and change over time. If knowledge communities are an important part of innovation, then there is value in considering how the rules and incentive structures of science and technology, the legal context, and the institutional context affect and promote knowledge communities. Academic research in science has strong norms that encourage knowledge sharing and collaboration; these norms are helpful in sustaining the exchange of information, the rapidity of change, and the character of knowledge communities. We believe, for example, that a mix of niche journals and some interdisciplinary journals does a better job of encouraging the development and quality of exchange than either interdisciplinary journals or niche journals alone. The development of lists of prestigious journals across disciplines that are used in tenure decisions is, from this perspective, negative for knowledge communities. The negative value of the coefficients in our findings for journal prestige implied that the more articles there are in a knowledge community that publishes in prestigious journals, the worse it does—though the positive coefficient for prestige on the individual level suggests that individuals are well served by publishing in such journals. This tension between individual and group incentives is interesting. Might a cross-temporal analysis of this tension find that this is an emerging trend and, if so, what are the consequences for knowledge communities? Recently, journals have been under enormous pressure in the sciences. Libraries ask for digital access, rather than paper copies, and researchers pay to publish, in some cases, to provide open-source work.

Government policies about innovation have long impacted patenting; indeed, patenting was conceptualized as a way to reward innovation by allowing innovators to derive benefits from their work. The U.S. Patent and Trademark Office is increasingly allowing patenting of more conceptual ideas, formulas, computer codes, and the like. The increase in strength of patenting in intellectual property is perhaps inevitable in an increasingly knowledge-driven economy, particularly with technical academic work being increasingly commercialized, but it poses a danger for knowledge communities. As knowledge becomes more proprietary, it is less likely to be shared as readily or as quickly. This may negatively impact the sharing and collaboration norms in knowledge communities in academic settings. Overall, open sharing in knowledge communities is valuable and useful in innovation and can function to encourage collaboration in complement to traditional firm structures; structures that discourage sharing should be given careful consideration.

WHAT KNOWLEDGE COMMUNITIES TELL US ABOUT FIRMS

Particularly for knowledge creation and innovation, there may be an essential division of labor between firm and non-firm forms of organization. We have found that the informal inter-firm organizations we call knowledge communities play an important role in these functions. In a world of competing institutional settings, an interaction between firm and non-firm forms of organization may be essential to creative endeavors, as Ronald Coase's work on transaction cost pointed out so well. We have speculated that firms are best at promoting cooperation, whereas knowledge communities are superior at promoting collaboration.

The idea of informal community-based collaboration vs. formal organizations based on arm's length business exchange, has deep roots in the sociological literature. Ferdinand Tonnies, in *Gemeinschaft und Gesellschaft* (1957), differentiated between social orders based primarily on the "natural will," natural inclination, or ways of life, and social orders based on the "rational will"—in other words, between self-interested exchange and ends-based behavior. In his distinction we see a parallel between "natural" knowledge communities, made up of researchers from different organizations tied together by their interest in similar things, having direct advantages in collaborating, and sharing innovations, and the more "rational" markets that are inclined towards instrumental exchanges dictating most transactions (Berg, Davidson, & Potts, 2019; Rindfleisch, 2020; Tsang, 2000; Williamson, 1979). Similarly, Durkheim (1997 [1893]) wrote about community organizations held together by homogeneity and forms of social organization based on heterogeneity (such as within-firm heterogeneity). He saw an irreversible historical trend away from mechanically solidarity societies that represented undifferentiated beliefs and conduct, and toward the organically solidarity societies, based on differentiated members and division of labor.

In their own ways, both Tonnies and Durkheim saw the transition from homogenous communities to heterogeneous rational exchange as a natural progression in social order. Why has scientific research been so resistant in transforming from *Gemeinschaft* to *Gesellschaft*? Why does science and research seem, in their social collaborative order but not their subjects, technology, or tools, to be so resistant to this change? Arguably, universities, a class of organization with very change-resistant norms that encourage knowledge sharing and interaction, have buffered science and technology from the transition, and perhaps innovation was more closely tied to these earlier norms. But perhaps knowledge communities remain intact because research is essentially not easy to bureaucratize, ideas are not easy to monetize, and creativity is not easy to commoditize. Innovation requires a wild magic that cannot be tamed or rationalized.

Firms, we argue, although they excel at encouraging ends-oriented cooperation, do not easily facilitate creative collaboration, an area where communities do excel. And collaboration, we have argued, rests at the heart of innovation and knowledge development. Going forward, we expect that areas of research that require intense innovation, creativity, and exploration will continue to support interorganizational communities between firms and research institutions. The direction of causality is not clear: Is research so community-based because communities are superior at collaboration and exploratory innovation, or is such research community-based because of its constituencies and the heavy influence of academic institutions? Perhaps both are true; perhaps radically exploratory research is best left to communities, and also academic institutions are culturally well placed for such research, somewhat buffering their members from pure *Gesellschaft*.

The future trends of such research are not clear either—will innovation move toward rationalization and more clearly into the rational tradition, or continue to be deeply community-based? The rise of Silicon Valley, and other hubs of community-based business, lead us to believe that non-academic forms of organizational structure, such as Porter's geographical clusters, may be able to sustain community-based innovation on a geographical dimension. Nevertheless, the proximity of Stanford reportedly had a lot to do with the initial emergence of Silicon Valley, as MIT and Harvard did with Route 66, and Duke, UNC Chapel Hill, and NC State did with the technology triangle in North Carolina. Perhaps, therefore, academic community-based organizations play an essential role here as well (Porter, 1998).

We believe that technology will continue to drive innovation in another direction as well. The digitalization of knowledge and knowledge sharing will mean that decentralized communities, like knowledge communities, DAOs, blockchains, or Web3, based on ideas and shared interests, will be increasingly important to exploratory innovation and knowledge creation (Rosenkopf & Tushman, 1998). Shared collaboration and exchange of ideas between researchers working on new ideas seem, to us, to most efficiently promote broad progress in scientific and technical progress.

We found evidence that knowledge communities are important drivers for innovation and receive, within their domains, a disproportionate share of citations in comparison with firms. In the computer science dataset, used in Chapter 2, 56.61% of citations were received by papers in clusters of knowledge communities, even though only 43.67% of papers were in clusters. This trend was much more extreme within clusters—76.16% of citations went from one paper in a cluster to another paper in a cluster. Papers not in a cluster, however, cited almost proportionately to the ratio of papers in and out of a cluster, with 41.32% of citations going to the 43.67% of papers in a cluster and 58.68% of citations going to the 56.33% of papers not in a cluster.

Research in the hard sciences and technical sciences is increasingly becoming interconnected with industry, as academic findings are commercialized and firms fund academic research (Gittelman, 2003; Gittelman & Kogut, 2003; Mowery & Shane, 2002; Shane, 2002). For example, we found that about 30% of the papers in our computer science dataset came from authors with industry affiliations. Knowledge communities in academic settings spur greater innovation, which spills over into industry and increases productivity and innovation throughout the economy.

Knowledge communities seem to be a meaningful element in how science and technology evolve. While formal organizations, like firms and governments, are easier to see and usually require explicit membership, knowledge communities allow people in based only on the way they interact with, and are received by, their peers; if the work of an innovator is influential, it will be central to that knowledge community. In *War and Peace*, Leo Tolstoy wrote about such parallel systems of order: "Boris now clearly understood—what he had already guessed—that side by side with the system of discipline and subordination which were laid down in the Army Regulations, there existed a different and more real system … Boris decided at once that he would be guided not by the official system but by this other unwritten system." Author and moralist C. S. Lewis, quoting Tolstoy in his essay "The Inner Ring" (2001 [1943]), goes on to argue that the important forms of group membership can transcend the formal social structures of prestigious clubs or professional titles (the exclusionary gangs he calls "inner rings") to include that sense of belonging, which is granted by collaborators that respect and use your work:

> If in your working hours you make the work your end, you will presently find yourself all unawares inside the only circle in your profession that really matters. You will be one of the sound craftsmen, and other sound craftsmen will know it. This group of craftsmen will by no means coincide with the Inner Ring or the Important People or the People in the Know. It will not shape that professional policy or work up that professional influence which fights for the profession as a whole against the

public: nor will it lead to those periodic scandals and crises which the Inner Ring produces. But it will do those things which that profession exists to do and will in the long run be responsible for all the respect which that profession in fact enjoys and which the speeches and advertisements cannot maintain.

We have argued that the structure of science and technology increasingly lies in knowledge communities, which promote collaboration and that shape the evolution of innovation. This insight, extended and developed, has implications for accelerating innovation in science in technology and impacting allocation in venture capital, blockchain, and R&D in startups. And the discovery of strong links between innovation rates and the existence and shape of knowledge communities also has fascinating policy implications for the public sector and resource allocation. In an increasingly digital and collaborative world, interorganizational knowledge communities are an essential conceptual framework, in addition to firms, technology hubs, and disruptive startups, for thinking about how innovation occurs and new ideas are developed in science and technology.

References

Abrahamson, E. (1996). Management fashion. *Academy of Management Review 21*(1): 254–85.

Abrahamson, E., & Piazza, A. (2019). The lifecycle of management ideas: innovation, diffusion, institutionalization, dormancy, and rebirth. In A. Sturdy, S. Heusinkveld, T. Reay, and D. Strang (Eds.), *The Oxford Handbook of Management Ideas* (pp. 42–67). Oxford: Oxford University Press.

Adner, R., & Levinthal, D. (2000). Technology speciation and the path of emerging technologies. In G. S. Day, P. J. H. Schoemaker, & R. E. Gunther (Eds.), *Wharton on Managing Emerging Technologies* (ch. 3). New York: John Wiley and Sons.

Afzali, A., Dimitrakopoulos, C., & Breen, T. (2002). High-performance, solution-processed organic thin film transistors from a novel pentacene precursor. *Journal of the American Chemical Society 124*(30): 8812–13.

Afzali, A., Dimitrakopoulos, C., & Graham, T. (2003). Photosensitive pentacene precursor: synthesis, photothermal patterning, and application in thin-film transistors. *Advanced Materials 15*(24): 2066–9.

Aharonson, B. S., Baum, J. A. C., & Feldman, M. P. (2004). Industrial clustering and the returns to inventive activity: Canadian biotechnology firms, 1991–2000. DRUID Working Papers 04-03, DRUID, Copenhagen Business School, Department of Industrial Economics and Strategy/Aalborg University, Department of Business Studies.

Aksom, H. (2021). Reconciling conflicting predictions about transience and persistence of management concepts in management fashion theory and new institutionalism. *International Journal of Organizational Analysis.* https://doi.org/10.1108/IJOA-10-2020-2445.

Albert, M. B., Avery, D., Narin, F., & McAllister, P. (1991). Direct validation of citation counts as indicators of industrially important patents. *Research Policy 20*(3): 251–9.

Ali, A., & Gittelman, M. (2016). Research paradigms and useful inventions in medicine: patents and licensing by teams of clinical and basic scientists in academic medical centers. *Research Policy 45*(8): 1499–511.

Amir, S. (1985). On the degree of interdisciplinarity of research programs—a quantitative assessment. *Scientometrics 8*(1–2): 117–36.

Antons, D., Grünwald, E., Cichy, P., & Salge, T. O. (2020). The application of text mining methods in innovation research: current state, evolution patterns, and development priorities. *R&D Management 50*(3): 329–51.

Arutyunov, V. V., & Medvedeva, I. E. (1992). Citation of scientific literature on geology. *Nauchno-Tekhnicheskaya Informatsiya Seriya 1-Organizatsiya I Metodika Informatsionnoi Raboty 9*: 24–30.

Barnett, W. P., & Sorenson, O. (2002). The Red Queen in organizational creation and development. *Industrial and Corporate Change 11*(2): 289–325.

Barney, J. (1986). Types of competition and the theory of strategy: towards an integrative framework. *Academy of Management Review 11*: 791–800.

Barney, J., Wright, M., & Ketchen, D. J. (2001). The resource-based view of the firm: ten years after 1991. *Journal of Management 27*(6): 625–41.

Bartel, C. A., & Saavedra, R. (2000). The collective construction of work group moods. *Administrative Science Quarterly 45*(2): 197–231.

Bastero-Gil, M., Freese, K., & Mersini-Houghton, L. (2003). What can WMAP tell us about the very early universe? New physics as an explanation of suppressed large scale power and running spectral index. *Physical Review D 68*: 123514.

Bayer, A. E., & Folger, J. (1966). Some correlates of a citation measure of productivity in science. *Sociology of Education 39*(4): 381–90.

Berg, C., Davidson, S., & Potts, J. (2019). Blockchain technology as economic infrastructure: revisiting the electronic markets hypothesis. *Frontiers in Blockchain 2*: 22.

Birnbaum, P. H. (1981a). Academic interdisciplinary research—characteristics of successful projects. *SRA—Journal of the Society of Research Administrators 13*(1): 5–16.

Birnbaum, P. H. (1981b). Integration and specialization in academic research. *Academy of Management Journal 24*(3): 487–503.

Birnbaum, P. H. (1981c). Contingencies for interdisciplinary research—matching research questions with research organizations. *Management Science 27*(11): 1279–93.

Blackburn, R. S. (1990). Organizational behavior—whom do we talk to and who talks to us? *Journal of Management 16*(2): 279–305.

Boyack, K. W., & Borner, K. (2003). Indicator-assisted evaluation and funding of research: visualizing the influence of grants on the number and citation counts of research papers. *Journal of the American Society for Information Science and Technology 54*(5): 447–61.

Braam, R. R., Moed, H. F., & Vanraan, A. F. J. (1988). Mapping of science: critical elaboration and new approaches, a case study in agricultural related biochemistry. In L. Egghe & R. Rousseau (Eds.), *Informetrics 89/90*.

Braam, R. R., Moed, H. F., & Vanraan, A. F. J. (1991a). Mapping of science by combined cocitation and word analysis. 1. Structural aspects. *Journal of the American Society for Information Science 42*(4): 233–51.

Braam, R. R., Moed, H. F., & Vanraan, A. F. J. (1991b). Mapping of science by combined cocitation and word analysis. 2. Dynamic aspects. *Journal of the American Society for Information Science 42*(4): 252–66.

Brown, J., & Duguid, P. (1991). Organizational learning and communities of practice. *Organization Science 2*(1): 40–57.

Brown, J., & Duguid, P. (2000). Knowledge and organization. *Organization Science 12*(2): 198–213.

Bürgi, L., Richards, T., Friend, R., & Sirringhaus, H. (2003). Close look at charge carrier injection in polymer field-effect transistors. *Journal of Applied Physics 94*(9): 6129–37.

Burt, R. (1977). Power in a social topology. *Social Science Research 6*(1): 1–83.

Burt, R. (1997). The contingent value of social capital. *Administrative Science Quarterly 42*(2), 339–65.

Burt, R. (2000). The network structure of social capital. *Research in Organizational Behavior 22*: 345–423.

Castro, P. L., & Lima, M. L. (2001). Old and new ideas about the environment and science: an exploratory study. *Environment & Behavior 33*(3): 400–423.

Chen, C. M., McCain, K., White, H., & Lin, X. (2002). Mapping *Scientometrics* (1981–2001). *ASIST 2002: Proceedings of the 65th ASIST Annual Meeting 39: 25–34.*

Chesterfield, R., Newman, C., Pappenfus, T., Ewbank, P., Haukaas, M., Mann, K., Miller, L., & Frisbie, C. (2003). High electron mobility and ambipolar transport in organic thin-film transistors based on a pi-stacking quinoidal terthiophene. *Advanced Materials 15*(15): 1278.

Choi, J. P. (2004). Tying and innovation: a dynamic analysis of tying arrangements. *The Economic Journal 114*(492): 83–101.

Choi, S. C., & Coughlan, A. T. (2006). Private label positioning: quality versus feature differentiation from the national brand. *Journal of Retailing 82*(2): 79–83.

Coe, R., & Weinstock, I. (1969). Evaluating journal publications: perceptions versus reality. *AACSB Bulletin 1*: 23–37.

Coe, R., & Weinstock, I. (1984). Evaluating the management journals: a 2nd look. *Academy of Management Journal 27*(3): 660–66.

Cohen, W. M., & Levinthal, D. A. (1990). Absorptive capacity—a new perspective on learning and innovation. *Administrative Science Quarterly 35*(1): 128–52.

Cohen, W. M., Nelson, R. R., & Walsh, J. P. (2000). Protecting their intellectual assets: appropriability conditions and why U.S. manufacturing firms patent (or not). *National Bureau of Economic Research Working Paper 7552*.

Cole, S., & Cole, J. R. (1967). Scientific output and recognition—a study in the operation of the reward system in science. *American Sociological Review 32*(3): 377–90.

Collins, G. P. (2004). Next stretch for plastic electronics. *Scientific American 291*(2): 74–81.

Collins, R. (1997). On social structure and science—Merton, RK. *American Journal of Sociology 103*(1): 275–8.

Crane, D. (1972). *Invisible Colleges: Diffusion of Knowledge in Scientific Communities.* Chicago: University of Chicago Press.

Crane, D. (1980). An exploratory study of Kuhnian paradigms in theoretical high energy physics. *Social Studies of Science 10*(1): 23–54.

Crane, D. (1989). How scientists communicate—a citation classic commentary on invisible-colleges—diffusion of knowledge in scientific communities by Crane, D. *Current Contents/Arts & Humanities 22*: 14.

Crick, F. (1988). *What Mad Pursuit: A Personal View of Scientific Discovery.* New York: Basic Books.

Cuhls, K. (2003). From forecasting to foresight processes—new participative foresight activities in Germany. *Journal of Forecasting 22*(2–3): 93–111.

Culnan, M. J. (1986). The intellectual development of management information-systems, 1972–1982: a co-citation analysis. *Management Science 32*(2): 156–72.

Culnan, M. J. (1987). Mapping the intellectual structure of MIS, 1980–1985: a co-citation analysis. *MIS Quarterly 11*(3): 341–53.

Culnan, M. J., O'Reilly, C. A., & Chatman, J. A. (1990). Intellectual structure of research in organizational behavior, 1972–1984: a co-citation analysis. *Journal of the American Society for Information Science 41*(6): 453–8.

Cupers, P., Orlans, I., Craessaerts, K., Annaert, W., & De Strooper, B. (2001). The amyloid precursor protein (APP)-cytoplasmic fragment generated by gamma-secretase is rapidly degraded but distributes partially in a nuclear fraction of neurones in culture. *Journal of Neurochemistry 78*(5): 1168–78.

Delgado, M., & Porter, M. E. (2021). Clusters and the great recession. *Available at SSRN 3819293.*

Diggle, P., Heagerty, P., Liang, K., & Zeger, S. (2002). *Analysis of Longitudinal Data.* Oxford: Oxford University Press.

DiMaggio, P. J., & Powell, W. W. (1983). The iron cage revisited—institutional isomorphism and collective rationality in organizational fields. *American Sociological Review 48*(2): 147–60.

Doreian, P. (1988). Testing structural-equivalence hypotheses in a network of geographical journals. *Journal of the American Society for Information Science 39*(2): 79–85.

Downs, A. (1957). *An Economic Theory of Democracy.* New York: Harper.

Drucker, P. F. (1985). *Innovation and Entrepreneurship: Practice and Principles.* New York: Harper & Row.

Drukker, D. M. (2003). Testing for serial correlation in linear panel-data models. *Stata Journal 3*(2): 168–77.

Durkheim, E. (1997 [1893]). *The Division of Labor in Society.* New York: Free Press.

Eccles, R. G., Nohria, N., & Berkley, J. D. (1992). *Beyond the Hype: Rediscovering the Essence of Management.* Boston: Harvard Business School Press.

Ennis, J. G. (1992). The social organization of sociological knowledge—modeling the intersection of specialties. *American Sociological Review 57*(2): 259–65.

Eriksen, H., Hansen, F., Banday, A., Gorski, K., & Lilje, P. (2004). Asymmetries in the cosmic microwave background anisotropy field. *Astrophysical Journal 605*(1): 14–20.

Extejt, M. M., & Smith, J. E. (1990). The behavioral sciences and management—an evaluation of relevant journals. *Journal of Management 16*(3): 539–51.

Facchetti, A., Deng, Y., Wang, A., Koide, Y., Sirringhaus, H., Marks, T., & Friend, R. (2000). Tuning the semiconducting properties of sexithiophene by alpha,omega-substitution—alpha,omega-diperfluorohexylsexithiophene: the first n-type sexithiophene for thin-film transistors. *Angewandte Chemie International Edition 39*(24): 4547.

Facchetti, A., Mushrush, M., Katz, H., & Marks, T. (2003). N-type building blocks for organic electronics: a homologous family of fluorocarbon-substituted thiophene oligomers with high carrier mobility. *Advanced Materials 15*(1): 33.

Facchetti, A., Yoon, M., Stern, C., Katz, H., & Marks, T. (2003). Building blocks for n-type organic electronics: regiochemically modulated inversion of majority carrier sign in perfluoroarene-modified polythiophene semiconductors. *Angewandte Chemie International Edition 42*(33): 3900–3903.

Falkingham, L. T., & Reeves, R. (1998). Context analysis—a technique for analysing research in a field, applied to literature on the management of R&D at the section level. *Scientometrics 42*(2): 97–120.

Fleming, L. (2001). Recombinant uncertainty in technological search. *Management Science 47*(1): 117–32.

Fleming, L., Mingo, S., & Chen, D. (2005). Brokerage versus cohesion and collaborative creativity: an evolutionary resolution (*draft*).

Fleming, L., & Sorenson, O. (2001). Technology as a complex adaptive system: evidence from patent data. *Research Policy 30*(7): 1019–39.

Garfield, E. (1983). How to use citation analysis for faculty evaluations, and when is it relevant? Part 2. *Current Contents* (45): 5–14.

Garfield, E. (1988). Information technology and the social sciences. *Current Contents 46*: 3–9.

Garfield, E., Pudovkin, A. I., & Istomin, V. S. (2003). Why do we need algorithmic historiography? *Journal of the American Society for Information Science and Technology 54*(5): 400–412.

Garfield, E., & Stevens, L. J. (1965). On the Science-Citation-Index (SCI) and related recent developments. *Nachrichten für Dokumentation 16*(3): 130–40.

Gasper, J. T. (2005). *Political news* [paper presentation]. Annual Meeting of the Public Choice Society.

Gelinck, G., Huitema, H., Van Veenendaal, E., Cantatore, E., Schrijnemakers, L., Van der Putten, J., Geuns, T., Beenhakkers, M., Giesbers, J., Huisman, B., Meijer, E., Benito, E., Touwslager, F., Marsman, A., Van Rens, B., & De Leeuw, D. (2004). Flexible active-matrix displays and shift registers based on solution-processed organic transistors. *Nature Materials 3*(2): 106–10.

Gerlach, M. L. (1992). The Japanese corporate network: a blockmodel analysis. *Administrative Science Quarterly* (March): 105–39.

Giest, S. (2021). Capacity concepts in cluster and innovation research. In *The Capacity to Innovate* (pp. 15–36). Toronto: University of Toronto Press.

Gittelman, M. (2003). Does geography matter for science-based firms? Epistemic communities and the geography of research and patenting in biotechnology. *Organization Science 18*(4): 724–41.

Gittelman, M., & Kogut, B. (2003). Does good science lead to valuable knowledge? Biotechnology firms and the evolutionary logic of citation patterns. *Management Science 49*(4): 366–82.

Gmur, M. (2003). Co-citation analysis and the search for invisible colleges: a methodological evaluation. *Scientometrics 57*(1): 27–57.

Gomezmejia, L. R., & Balkin, D. B. (1992). Determinants of faculty pay: an agency theory perspective. *Academy of Management Journal 35*(5): 921–55.

Gottschlich, N., Jacobson, S., Culbertson, C., & Ramsey, J. (2001). Two-dimensional electrochromatography/capillary electrophoresis on a microchip. *Analytical Chemistry 73*(11): 2669–74.

Granovetter, M. (1994). Business groups. In N. Smelser and R. Swedberg (Eds.). *Handbook of Economic Sociology* (pp. 453–75). Princeton: Princeton University Press.

Gugarati, D. (1995). *Basic Econometrics* (3rd edn.). New York: McGraw-Hill.

Guha, S. M., Meyerson, A., Mishra, N., Motwana, R., & O'Callaghan, L. (2003). Clustering data streams: theory and practice. Unpublished manuscript. https://theory.stanford.edu/~nmishra/Papers/clusteringDataStreamsTheoryPractice.pdf.

Guimera, R., Uzzi, B., Spiro, J., & Amaral, L. (2005). Team assembly mechanisms determine collaboration network structure and team performance. *Science 308*(29): 697–702.

Gulovsen, E. (2019). International science and US military capability: global innovation ecosystems and US industry. *Phalanx 52*(4): 26–33.

Hagedoorn, J., & Duysters, G. (2002). Learning in dynamic inter-firm networks—the efficacy of multiple contacts. *Organizational Studies 23*(4): 525–48.

Halik, M., Klauk, H., Zschieschang, U., Schmid, G., Ponomarenko, S., Kirchmeyer, S., & Weber, W. (2003). Relationship between molecular structure and electrical performance of oligothiophene organic thin film transistors. *Advanced Materials 15*(11): 917–22.

Hargens, L. L. (2000a). Graphing micro-regions in the web of knowledge: a comparative reference-network analysis. In B. Cronin & H. Atkins (Eds.), *The Web of Knowledge—A Festschrift in Honor of Eugene Garfield* (pp. 497–516). Medford: American Society for Information Science.

Hargens, L. L. (2000b). Using the literature: reference networks, reference contexts, and the social structure of scholarship. *American Sociological Review 65*(6): 846–65.

Hassan, E. (2003). Simultaneous mapping of interactions between scientific and technological knowledge bases: The case of space communications. *Journal of the American Society for Information Science and Technology 54*(5): 462–8.

Hausman, J. A., Hall, B. H., & Griliches, Z. (1984). Econometric models for count data with an application to the patents–R&D relationship. National Bureau of Economic Research, Technical Working Paper Series 17. DOI 10.3386/t0017.

Haynes, A., Lackman, C., & Guskey, A. (1999). Comprehensive brand presentation: ensuring consistent brand image. *Journal of Product and Brand Management 8*(4): 28–30.

Henderson, R. M., & Clark, K. B. (1990). Architectural innovation: the reconfiguration of existing product technologies and the failure of established firms. *Administrative Science Quarterly 35*(1): 9–30.

Henderson, R., Jaffe, A. B., & Trajtenberg, M. (1998). Universities as a source of commercial technology: a detailed analysis of university patenting, 1965–1988. *Review of Economics and Statistics 80*(1): 119–27.

Hotelling, H. (1929). Stability in competition. *Economic Journal 39*(153): 41–57.

Hsu, L.-Y., Lee, C.-C., Green, J. A., Ang, B., Paton, N. I., Lee, L., Villacian, J. S., Lim, P.-L., Earnest, A., & Leo, Y.-S. (2003). Severe Acute Respiratory Syndrome (SARS) in Singapore: clinical features of index patient and initial contacts. *Emerging Infectious Diseases 9*(6): 713–17.

Hurley, R. F., & Hult, G. T. M. (1998). Innovation, market orientation, and organizational learning: an integration and empirical examination. *Journal of Marketing 62*(3): 42–54.

Hwang, E. H., Singh, P. V., & Argote, L. (2015). Knowledge sharing in online communities: learning to cross geographic and hierarchical boundaries. *Organization Science 26*(6): 1593–611.

Jacobs, A. Z., & Watts, D. J. (2021). A large-scale comparative study of informal social networks in firms. *Management Science*. https://pubsonline.informs.org/doi/10.1287/mnsc.2021.3997.

Jaffe, A. B., & Lerner, J. (2001). Reinventing public R&D: patent policy and the commercialization of national laboratory technologies. *RAND Journal of Economics 32*(1): 167–98.

Jayaraj, S., & Gittelman, M. (2017). Searching with maps: impact of the human genome project on drug discovery. *Academy of Management Proceedings*. DOI:10.5465/AMBPP.2017.14608abstract.

Jayaraj, S., & Gittelman, M. (2018a). Impact of scientific maps on technological search and novelty. *Academy of Management Proceedings 1*: 15414.

Jayaraj, S., & Gittelman, M. (2018b). Scientific breakthroughs and patent scope: the impact of the human genome project on early stage drug patents [paper presentation]. 78th Annual Meeting of the Academy of Management.

Johnson, J. L., & Podsakoff, P. M. (1994). Journal influence in the field of management—an analysis using Salancik's index in a dependency network. *Academy of Management Journal 37*(5): 1392–407.

Jones, B. F. (2021). The rise of research teams: benefits and costs in economics. *Journal of Economic Perspectives 35*(2): 191–216.

Jung, Y., Kim, E., & Kim, W. (2019). The scientific and technological interdisciplinary research of government research institutes: network analysis of the innovation cluster in South Korea. *Policy Studies 42*: 1–20.

Kandylas, B. (2005). A mixture model for document clustering by citations. Unpublished manuscript.

Kandylas, V., Ungar, L. H., & Forster, D. (2005). Winner-take-all EM clustering. Unpublished paper, University of Pennsylvania.

Katila, R. (2002). New product search overtime: past ideas in their prime? *Academy of Management Journal 45*(5): 995–1010.

Katila, R. (2005). *Innovative product portfolios by navigating markets and technology*. Working paper. Department of Management Science and Engineering, Terman Engineering Center, Stanford University.

Katila, R., & Ahuja, G. (2002). Something old, something new: a longitudinal study of search behavior and new product introduction. *Academy of Management Journal 45*(6): 1183–94.

Kerr, W. R., & Robert-Nicoud, R. (2020). Tech clusters. *Journal of Economic Perspectives 34*(3): 50–76.

Khoury, J., Ovrut, B., Seiberg, N., Steinhardt, P., & Turok, N. (2002). From big crunch to big bang. *Physical Review D 65*(8): 6007.

Khoury, J., Ovrut, B., Steinhardt, P., & Turok, N. (2001). Ekpyrotic universe: colliding branes and the origin of the hot big bang. *Physical Review D 64*(12): 3522.

Kirkpatrick, S. A., & Locke, E. A. (1992). The development of measures of faculty scholarship. *Group and Organization Management 17*(1): 5–23.

Kogut, B., & Macpherson, J. M. (2004). The decision to privatize as an economic policy idea: epistemic communities, palace wars, and diffusion. Unpublished manuscript.

Kolbjørnsrud, V. (2017). Agency problems and governance mechanisms in collaborative communities. *Strategic Organization 15*(2): 141–73.

Kripke, S. (1982). *Wittgenstein in Rules and Private Language*. Cambridge, MA: Harvard University Press.

Krishna, R. V. (2001). Voter clustering and the theory of spacial voting with entry. Unpublished manuscript.

Kuhn, T. (1962). *The Structure of Scientific Revolutions*. Chicago and London: University of Chicago Press.

Leahey, E., Beckman, C. M., & Stanko, T. L. (2017). Prominent but less productive: the impact of interdisciplinarity on scientists' research. *Administrative Science Quarterly 62*(1): 105–39.

Leem, J., Vijayan, S., Han, P., Cai, D., Machura, M., Lopes, K., Veselits, M., Xu, H., & Thinakaran, G. (2002). Presenilin 1 is required for maturation and cell surface accumulation of nicastrin. *Journal of Biological Chemistry 277*(21): 19236–40.

Leissring, M., Murphy, M., Mead, T., Akbari, Y., Sugarman, M., Jannatipour, M., Anliker, B., Muller, U., Saftig, P., De Strooper, B., Wolfe, M., Golde, T., & LaFerla, F. (2002). A physiologic signaling role for the gamma-secretase-derived intracellular fragment of APP. *Proceedings of the National Academy of Sciences of the United States of America 99*(7): 4697–702.

Lenk, P. (1983). Mappings of fields based on nominations. *Journal of the American Society for Information Science 34*(2): 115–22.

Levinthal, D. A. (1991). Organizational adaptation and environmental selection—interrelated processes of change. *Organization Science 2*: 140–45.

Levinthal, D. A. (1997). Adaptation on rugged landscapes. *Management Science 43*(7): 934–50.

Levinthal, D. A. (1998). The slow pace of rapid technological change: gradualism and punctuation in technological change. *Industrial & Corporate Change 7*(2): 217–47.

Levinthal, D. A., & March, J. G. (1981). A model of adaptive organizational search. *Journal of Economic Behavior & Organization 2*(4): 307–33.

Levinthal, D. A., & Warglien, M. (1999). Landscape design: designing for local action in complex worlds. *Organization Science 10*(3): 342–57.

Lewis, C. S. (2001 [1943]). The inner ring. In *The Weight of Glory: And Other Addresses.* New York: HarperCollins.

Lieberman, M. B., & Montgomery, D. B. (1988). First-mover advantages. *Strategic Management Journal 9* (Special Issue): 41–58.

Lim, M., & Ong, B. Y. (2019). Communities of innovation. *International Journal of Innovation Science 11*(3): 402–18.

Liu, R., Stremler, M., Sharp, K., Olsen, M., Santiago, J., Adrian, R., Aref, H., & Beebe, D. (2000). Passive mixing in a three-dimensional serpentine microchannel. *Journal of Microelectromechanical Systems 9*(2): 190–97.

Lodahl, J. B., & Gordon, G. (1972). The structure of scientific fields and the functioning of university graduate departments. *American Sociological Review 37*: 57–72.

Long, J. S. (1997). *Regression Models for Categorical and Limited Dependent Variables*. Thousand Oaks: Sage Publications.

Lyth, D. (2002). The primordial curvature perturbation in the ekpyrotic universe. *Physics Letters B 524*(1–2): 1–4.

Ma, Y., & Uzzi, B. (2018). Scientific prize network predicts who pushes the boundaries of science. *Proceedings of the National Academy of Sciences of the United States of America 115*(50): 12608–15.

Makadok, R. (1998). Can first-mover and early-mover advantages be sustained in an industry with low barriers to entry/imitation? *Strategic Management Journal 19*(7): 683–96.

March, J. G. (1991). Exploration and exploitation in organizational learning. *Organization Science 2*(1): 71–87.

March, J. G., & Shapira, Z. (1987). Managerial perspectives on risk and risk taking. *Management Science 33*(11): 1404–18.

March, J. G., & Simon, H. A. (1958). *Organizations*. New York: Wiley.

March, J. G., & Sutton, R. I. (1997). Organizational performance as a dependent variable. *Organization Science 8*(6): 698–706.

Marks, U. G., & Albers, S. (2001). Experiments in competitive product positioning: actual behavior compared to Nash solutions. *Schmalenbach Business Review 53*: 150–74.

Martin, J., Peter, P., Pinto-Neto, N., & Schwarz, D. J. (2002). Passing through the bounce in the ekpyrotic models. *Physical Review D 65*(12): 3513.

McCain, K. W. (1986a). Cross-disciplinary citation patterns in the history of technology. *Proceedings of the American Society for Information Science 23*: 194–8.

McCain, K. W. (1986b). The paper trails of scholarship: mapping the literature of genetics. *Library Quarterly 56*(3): 258–71.

McCain, K. W. (1987). Citation patterns in the history of technology. *Library & Information Science Research 9*(1): 41–59.

McCloskey, D. N. (1998). *The Rhetoric of Economics*. Madison: University of Wisconsin Press.

McGann, A. J. (2002). The advantages of ideological cohesion. *Journal of Theoretical Politics 14*(1): 37–70.

Merton, R. K. (1965). *On the Shoulders of Giants: A Shandean Postscript*. New York: Free Press.

Merton, R. K. (1968). *Social Theory and Social Structure*. New York: Free Press.

Merton, R. K. (1972). *The Sociology of Science*. Chicago: University of Chicago Press.

Meyer, M. W. (1994). Measuring performance in economic organizations. In N. J. Smelser and R. Swedberg (Eds.), *The Handbook of Economic Sociology* (pp. 556–80). Princeton: Princeton University Press, Russell Sage Foundation.

Meyer, M. W. (1999). Notes from a border discipline: has the border become the center? *Contemporary Sociology—A Journal of Reviews 28*(5): 507–10.

Meyer, M. W., & Zucker, L. G. (1989). *Permanently Failing Organizations*. Newbury Park: Sage Publications.

Milgram, S. (1967). The small world problem. *Psychology Today 2*: 60–67.

Milman, B. L., & Gavrilova, Y. A. (1993). Analysis of citation and cocitation in chemical-engineering. *Scientometrics 27*(1): 53–74.

Min, C., Bu, Y., & Sun, J. (2021). Predicting scientific breakthroughs based on knowledge structure variations. *Technological Forecasting and Social Change 164*: 120502.

Mintzberg, H. (1994). *The Rise and Fall of Strategic Planning*. New York and Toronto: Free Press.

Mizruchi, M. S., & Fein, L. C. (1999). The social construction of organizational knowledge: a study of the uses of coercive, mimetic, and normative isomorphism. *Administrative Science Quarterly 44*(4): 653–83.

Moody, J. (2001). Peer influence groups: identifying dense clusters in large networks. *Social Networks 23*(4): 261–83.

Morris, M. W., & Moore, P. C. (2000). The lessons we (don't) learn: counterfactual thinking and organizational accountability after a close call. *Administrative Science Quarterly 45*(4): 737–65.

Mowery, D. C., & Shane, S. (2002). Introduction to the special issue on university entrepreneurship and technology transfer. *Management Science 48*(1): v–ix.

Murphy, A., Frechet, J., Chang, P., Lee, J., & Subramanian, V. (2004). Organic thin film transistors from a soluble oligothiophene derivative containing thermally removable solubilizing groups. *Journal of the American Chemical Society 126*(6): 1596–7.

Murray, F. (2005). Exchange relationships & cumulative innovation: standing on the shoulders of the oncomouse. Unpublished manuscript.

Murray, F., & Stern, S. (2005). Do formal intellectual property rights hinder the free flow of scientific knowledge? [paper presentation]. NBER Academic Science and Entrepreneurship Conference.

Mushrush, M., Facchetti, A., Lefenfeld, M., Katz, H., & Marks, T. (2003). Easily processable phenylene-thiophene-based organic field-effect transistors and solution-fabricated nonvolatile transistor memory elements. *Journal of the American Chemical Society 125*(31): 9414–23.

Narin, F., Hamilton, K. S., & Olivastro, D. (1997). The increasing linkage between U.S. technology and public science. *Research Policy 26*(3): 317–30.

Nerkar, A. (2003). Old is gold? The value of temporal exploration in the creation of new knowledge. *Management Science 49*(2): 211–29.

Niemann, H., Moehrle, M. G., & Frischkorn, J. (2017). Use of a new patent text-mining and visualization method for identifying patenting patterns over time: concept, method and test application. *Technological Forecasting and Social Change 115*: 210–20.

Nohria, N., & Garcia-Pont, C. (1991). Global strategic linkages and industry structure. *Strategic Management Journal 12*: 105–24.

Oromaner, M. (1981). Articles in core economic journals—a citation analysis. *Knowledge: Creation, Diffusion, Utilization 3*(1): 83–96.

Osareh, F. (1996). Bibliometrics, citation analysis and co-citation analysis: a review of literature. Part 2. *Libri 46*(4): 217–25.

Pakes, A., & Shankerman, M. (1984). The rate of obsolescence of patents, research gestation lags, and the private rate of return to research resources. In Z. Griliches (Ed.), *R & D, Patents, and Productivity. A National Bureau of Economic Research Conference Report* (pp. 339–74). Chicago: University of Chicago Press.

Pantel, P., & Lin, D. (2002). Document clustering with committees [paper presentation]. Association for Computing Machinery's Special Interest Group on Information Retrieval, Tampere, Finland.

Parker, J. N., & Corte, U. (2017). Placing collaborative circles in strategic action fields: explaining differences between highly creative groups. *Sociological Theory 35*(4): 261–87.

Pedraza-Fariña, L. G., & Whalen, R. (2020). A network theory of patentability. *University of Chicago Law Review 87*(1): 63–144.

Peiris, J. S. M., Lai, S. T., Poon, L. L. M., Guan, Y., Yam, L. Y. C., Lim, W., et al. (2003). Coronavirus as a possible cause of severe acute respiratory syndrome. *Lancet 361*(9366): 1319–25.

Pfeffer, J. (1993). Barriers to the advance of organizational science: paradigm development as a dependent variable. *Academy of Management Review 18*(4): 599–620.

Phelps, J., & Johnson, E. (1996). Entering the quagmire: examining the "meaning" of integrated marketing communications. *Journal of Marketing Communications 2*(3): 159–72.

Piazza, A., & Abrahamson, E. (2020). Fads and fashions in management practices: taking stock and looking forward. *International Journal of Management Reviews 22*(3): 264–86.

Podolny, J. M., & Stuart, T. E. (1995). A role-based ecology of technological change. *American Journal of Sociology 100*(5): 1224–60.

Podsakoff, P. M., MacKenzie, S. B., Bachrach, D. G., & Podsakoff, N. P. (2005). The influence of management journals in the 1980s and 1990s. *Strategic Management Journal 26*: 473–88.

Podzorov, V., Sysoev, S., Loginova, E., Pudalov, V., & Gershenson, M. (2003). Single-crystal organic field effect transistors with the hole mobility similar to 8 cm(2)/V s. *Applied Physics Letters 83*(17): 3504–6.

Ponzi, L. J. (2002). The intellectual structure and interdisciplinary breadth of knowledge management: a bibliometric study of its early stage of development. *Scientometrics 55*(2): 259–72.

Popescul, A., Flake, G. W., Lawrence, S, Ungar, L. H., & Giles, L. C. (2000). Clustering and identifying temporal trends in document databases [paper presentation]. IEEE Advances in Digital Libraries, Washington, D.C.

Porter, M. E. (1985). *Competitive Advantage: Creating and Sustaining Superior Performance.* New York, London: Free Press, Collier Macmillan.

Porter, M. E. (1998). Clusters and the new economics of competition. *Harvard Business Review* (November–December): 77–90.

Porter, M. E., Ketels, C., Miller, K., & Bryden, R. (2004). *Competitiveness in Rural U.S. Regions: Learning and Research Agenda.* Washington, D.C.: Economic Development Administration.

Powell, W. W., Kogut, K. W., & Smith-Doerr, L. (1996). Interorganizational collaboration and the locus of innovation: networks of learning in biotechnology. *Administrative Science Quarterly 41*(1): 116–45.

Price, D. D. (1961). *Science Since Babylon*. New Haven: Yale University Press.

Price, D. D. (1963). *Big Science, Little Science*. New York: Columbia University Press.

Ramos-Rodriguez, A. R., & Ruiz-Navarro, J. (2004). Changes in the intellectual structure of strategic management research: a bibliometric study of the *Strategic Management Journal*, 1980–2000. *Strategic Management Journal 25*(10): 981–1004.

Reagans, R., Zuckerman, E., & McEvily, B. (2004). How to make the team: social networks vs. demography as criteria for designing effective teams. *Administrative Science Quarterly 49*: 101–33.

Rindfleisch, A. (2020). Transaction cost theory: past, present and future. *AMS Review*: 85–97.

Rosenkopf, L., & Nerkar, A. (2001). Beyond local search: boundary-spanning, exploration, and impact in the optical disk industry. *Strategic Management Journal 22*(4): 287–306.

Rosenkopf, L., & Tushman, M. L. (1998). The coevolution of community networks and technology: lessons from the flight simulation industry. *Academy of Management Journal 40*(5): 1150–74.

Rota, P. A., Oberste, M. S., Monroe, S. S., Nix, W. A., Campagnoli, R., Icenogle, J. P., Penaranda, S., Bankamp, B., Maher, K., Chen, M.-H., Tong, S., Tamin, A., Lowe, L., Frace, M., DeRisi, J. L., Chen, Q., Wang, D., Erdman, D. D., Peret, T. C. T., Burns, C., Ksiazek, T. G., Rollin, P. E., Sanchez, A., Liffick, S., Holloway, B., Limor, J., McCaustland, K., Olsen-Rasmussen, M., Fouchier, R., Gunther, S., Osterhaus, A. D. M. E., Drosten, C., Pallansch, M. A., Anderson, L. J., & Bellini, W. J. (2003). Characterization of a novel coronavirus associated with Severe Acute Respiratory Syndrome. *Science 300*(5624): 1394–9.

Rousseau, R., & Small, H. G. (2006). Escher staircases dwarfed. *ISSI Newsletter 1*(4): 8–10.

Ruan, Y., Wei, C., Ee, L., Vega, V., Thoreau, H., Yun, S., Chia, J., Ng, P., Chiu, K., Lim, L., Tao, Z., Peng, C., Ean, L., Lee, N., Sin, L., Ng, L., Chee, R., Stanton, L., Long, P., & Liu, E. (2003). Comparative full-length genome sequence analysis of 14 SARS coronavirus isolates and common mutations associated with putative origins of infection. *Lancet 361*(9371): 1779–85.

Salancik, G. R. (1986). An index of subgroup influence in dependency networks. *Administrative Science Quarterly 31*(2): 194–211.

Schardosin, F. Z., Del Rolt, C. R., Batista, A. M. L., Penz, D., Amorin, B., & Bier, C. A. (2020). Inter-organizational collaborative networks: a systematic review. 2020 International Conference on Technology and Entrepreneurship-Virtual (ICTE-V), IEEE: 1–8.

Schultz, D. E., Tannenbaum, S. I., & Lauterborn, R. F. (1994). *The New Marketing Paradigm: Integrated Marketing*. Chicago: NTC Business Books.

Schumpeter, J. A. (1934). *The Theory of Economic Development: An Inquiry into Profits, Capital, Credit, Interest, and the Business Cycle*. Cambridge, MA: Harvard University Press.

Shane, S. (2002). Selling university technology: patterns from MIT. *Management Science 48*(1): 122–37.

Sharplin, A. D., & Mabry, R. H. (1985). The relative importance of journals used in management research: an alternative ranking. *Human Relations 38*(2): 139–49.

Sheraw, C., Jackson, T., Eaton, D., & Anthony, J. (2003). Functionalized pentacene active layer organic thin-film transistors. *Advanced Materials 15*(23): 2009–11.

Siggelkow, N. (2001). Who reads my paper anyways? A survey of journal readership and reputation. *Wharton School, University of Pennsylvania working paper*.

Sisodia, S. S., & St. George-Hyslop, P. H. (2002). Gamma-Secretase, Notch, A Beta and Alzheimer's disease: where do the presenilins fit in? *Nature Reviews Neuroscience 3*(4): 281–90.

Slater, S. F., & Narver, J. C. (1995). Market orientation and the learning organization. *Journal of Marketing 59* (July): 63–74.

Small, H. G. (1976). Structural dynamics of scientific literature. *International Classification 3*(2): 67–74.

Small, H. G. (1977). Co-citation model of a scientific specialty—longitudinal-study of collagen research. *Social Studies of Science 7*(2): 139–66.

Small, H. G. (1978). Cited documents as concept symbols. *Social Studies of Science 8*(3): 327–40.

Small, H. G. (1992). Cogitations on cocitation: a citation-classic commentary on cocitation in scientific literature—new relationship between 2 documents by Small, H. *Current Contents/Social & Behavioral Sciences 10*: 10.

Small, H. G. (1994). A SCI-map case study: building a map of AIDS research. *Scientometrics 30*: 229–41.

Small, H. G. (1997). Update on science mapping: creating large document spaces. *Scientometrics 38*(2): 275–93.

Small, H. G. (1998). Citations and consilience in science—comments on theories of citation? *Scientometrics 43*(1): 143–8.

Small, H. G. (1999). A passage through science: crossing disciplinary boundaries. *Library Trends 48*(1): 72–108.

Small, H. G. (2003). Paradigms, citations, and maps of science: a personal history. *Journal of the American Society for Information Science and Technology 54*(5): 394–9.

Small, H. G. (2004). Why authors think their papers are highly cited. *Scientometrics 60*(3): 305–16.

Small, H. G. (2006). Tracking and predicting growth areas in science. *Scientometrics 68*(3): 595–610.

Small, H. G. (2018a). Characterizing highly cited method and non-method papers using citation contexts: the role of uncertainty. *Journal of Informetrics 12*(2): 461–80.

Small, H. G. (2018b). Citation indexing revisited: Garfield's early vision and its implications for the future. *Frontiers in Research Metrics and Analytics 3*(8).

Small, H. G., & Crane, D. (1979). Specialties and disciplines in science and social-science: an examination of their structure using citation indexes. *Scientometrics 1*(5–6): 445–61.

Small, H. G., & Greenlee, E. (1990). A co-citation study of AIDS research. In C. L. Borgman (Ed.), *Scientometrics* (pp. 166–93). Newbury Park, London, and New Delhi: Sage Publications.

Small, H. G., & Griffith, B. C. (1974). The structure of scientific literatures I: identifying and graphing specialties. *Science Studies 4*(1), 17–40.

Small, H. G., & Sweeney, E. (1985). Clustering the Science Citation Index using co-citations. I. Comparison of methods. *Scientometrics 7*(3–6): 391–409.

Small, H. G., & Upham, P. (2009). Citation structure of an emerging research area on the verge of application. *Scientometrics 79*(2): 365–75.

Steinhardt, P. J., & Turok, N. (2002). Cosmic evolution in a cyclic universe. *Physical Review D 65*(12): 6003.

Stigler, G. J., Stigler, S. M., & Friedland, C. (1995). The journals of economics. *Journal of Political Economy 103*(2): 331–59.

Stuart, H., & Kerr, G. (1999). Marketing communication and corporate identity: are they integrated? *Journal of Marketing Communications 5*(4): 169–79.

Sullivan, D., White, D. H., & Barboni, E. J. (1977). Co-citation analyses of science: an evaluation. *Social Studies of Science 7*(2) (Theme Issue: Citation Studies of Scientific Specialties): 223–40.

Sytch, M., & Tatarynowicz, A. (2014). Exploring the locus of invention: the dynamics of network communities and firms' invention productivity. *Academy of Management Journal 57*(1): 249–79.

Tegmark, M., de Oliveira-Costa, A., & Hamilton, A. J. S. (2003). High resolution foreground cleaned CMB map from WMAP. *Physical Review D 6812*(12): 3523.

Tonnies, F. (1957). *Gemeinschaft und Gesellschaft*. East Lansing: Michigan State University Press.

Tortoriello, M., McEvily, B., & Krackhardt, D. (2015). Being a catalyst of innovation: the role of knowledge diversity and network closure. *Organization Science 26*(2): 423–38.

Trajtenberg, M. (1990). A penny for your quotes: patent citations and the value of innovations. *RAND Journal of Economics 21*(1): 172–87.

Travers, J., & Milgram, S. (1969). An experimental study of the small world problem. *Sociometry 32*: 425–43.

Tsai, W. (2002). Social structure of "coopetition" within a multiunit organization: coordination, competition, and interorganizational knowledge sharing. *Organization Science 13*(2): 179–90.

Tsang, E. W. K. (2000). Transaction cost and resource-based explanations of joint ventures: a comparison and synthesis. *Organization Studies 21*(1): 215–42.

Upham, S. P. (2006). Communities of innovation: three essays on new knowledge development, PhD dissertation, University of Pennsylvania.

Upham, S. P., Rosenkopf, L., & Ungar, L. H. (2010a). Innovating knowledge communities: an analysis of group collaboration and competition in science and technology. *Scientometrics 83*(2): 525–54.

Upham, S. P., Rosenkopf, L., & Ungar, L. H. (2010b). Positioning knowledge: schools of thought and new knowledge creation. *Scientometrics 83*(2): 555–81.

Upham, S., & Small, H. G. (2010). Emerging research fronts in science and technology: patterns of new knowledge development. *Scientometrics 83*(1): 15–38.

Üsdiken, B., & Pasadeos, Y. (1995). Organizational analysis in North America and Europe: a comparison of cocitation networks. *Organization Studies 16*(3): 503–26.

Uzzi, B., & Spiro, J. (2005). Collaboration and creativity: the small world problem. *American Journal of Sociology 111*(2): 447–504.

Uzzi, B., Spiro, J., & Delis, D. (2005). Emergence: the origin and evolution of career networks in the Broadway musical industry, 1877–1995. Working paper, Kellogg School of Management.

Videlot, C., Ackermann, J., Blanchard, P., Raimundo, J. M., Frere, P., Allain, M., de Bettignies, R., Levillain, E., & Roncali, J. (2003). Field-effect transistors based on oligothienylenevinylenes: from solution pi-dimers to high-mobility organic semiconductors. *Advanced Materials 15*(4): 306–10.

Watts, D. J. (1999). Networks, dynamics, and the small-world phenomenon. *American Journal of Sociology 105*(2): 493–527.

Wenger, E. (1998). *Communities of Practice: Learning, Meaning and Identity*. Cambridge: Cambridge University Press.

Wernerfelt, B. (1984). A resource-based view of the firm. *Strategic Management Journal 5*(2): 171–80.

White, H. D. (2003). Pathfinder networks and author cocitation analysis: a remapping of paradigmatic information scientists. *Journal of the American Society for Information Science and Technology 54*(5): 423–34.

Williamson, O. E. (1975). *Markets and Hierarchies, Analysis and Antitrust Implications: A Study in the Economics of Internal Organization*. New York: Free Press.

Williamson, O. E. (1979). Transaction-cost economics: the governance of contractual relations. *Journal of Law & Economics 22*(2): 233–61.

Williamson, O. E. (1988). The logic of economic organization. *Journal of Law Economics & Organization 4*(1): 65–93.

Williamson, O. E. (2017). The economics and sociology of organization: promoting a dialogue. In G. Farkas & P. England (Eds.), *Industries, Firms, and Jobs* (pp. 159–86). New York: Routledge.

Wooldridge, J. M. (2002). *Econometric Analysis of Cross Section and Panel Data*. Cambridge, MA: MIT Press.

Yoels, W. C. (1974). Structure of scientific fields and allocation of editorships on scientific journals: some observations on politics of knowledge. *Sociological Quarterly 15*(2): 264–76.

Zhang, S., Zhang, N., Zhu, S., & Liu, F. (2020). A foot in two camps or your undivided attention? The impact of intra- and inter-community collaboration on firm innovation performance. *Technology Analysis & Strategic Management 32*(7): 753–68.

Zhong, S., & Ghosh, J. (2003). A comparative study of generative models for document clustering. In *Proceedings of the workshop on clustering high dimensional data and its applications in SIAM data mining conference*.

Index